Preparing for the Worst

Preparing for the Worst

A COMPREHENSIVE GUIDE TO
PROTECTING YOUR FAMILY FROM
TERRORIST ATTACKS, NATURAL
DISASTERS, AND OTHER
CATASTROPHES

James (Jay) Schaefer-Jones

PRAEGER SECURITY INTERNATIONAL
Westport, Connecticut · London

Library of Congress Cataloging-in-Publication Data

Schaefer-Jones, James.
  Preparing for the worst : a comprehensive guide to protecting your
family from terrorist attacks, natural disasters, and other
catastrophes / James (Jay) Schaefer-Jones.
      p. cm.
  Includes bibliographical references and index.
  ISBN-13: 978-0-275-99631-4 (alk. paper)
  ISBN-10: 0-275-99631-X (alk. paper)
  1.   Emergency management—United States—Handbooks, manuals, etc. 2.
Natural disasters—United States—Handbooks, manuals, etc. 3.   Weapons
of mass destruction—Safety measures—Handbooks, manuals, etc. 4.
Terrorism—United States—Handbooks, manuals, etc. I. Title.
  T55.3.H3S33 2007
  613.6'9—dc22   2007008639

British Library Cataloguing-in-Publication data is available.

Library of Congress Catalog Card Number: 2007008639
ISBN-13: 978-0-275-99631-4
ISBN-10: 0-275-99631-X

First published in 2007

Praeger Security International, 88 Post Road West, Westport, CT 06881
An imprint of Greenwood Publishing Group Inc.
www.praeger.com

Printed in the United States of America

The paper used in this book complies with the
Permanent Paper Standard issued by the National
Information Standards Organization (Z39.48-1984).

10   9   8   7   6   5   4   3   2   1

Contents

Tables and Figures

TABLES

FIGURES

Preface

Some of us have experienced disaster and its effects firsthand. Many more Americans have not. We live in an uncertain world, and the news media brings the proof into our homes every day. We see human tragedy so often that we may be desensitized to it because these events usually happen to someone else. We do not like to dwell on unpleasant thoughts, and sometimes, our human nature leads us into a state of denial: "I live in a safe, quiet neighborhood and these catastrophes will not happen to me and my family." Too often, we are content to live in the here and now with little thought about what tomorrow may bring unexpectedly. Frankly, it takes a significant effort to plan for an unpredictable future. Your primary responsibility is to protect your family, and this guide will help you to prepare.

In the event of a disaster, local government authorities, disaster-relief organizations, and public health departments will try to help you, but each family and community must also take steps to prepare. Emergency responders may not be able to reach you immediately, or they may need to focus their efforts elsewhere. Ultimately, it is up to you to protect your family. This guide explains different types of disasters (natural and man-made), suggests protective measures for you and your family, and offers sources of additional information.

Community involvement is an important part of disaster preparedness. To help your community prepare for and recover from a disaster, get involved and consider completing an American Red Cross First Aid or CPR course, or joining your local Volunteer First-Aid Squad, Volunteer Fire Department, or Community Emergency Response Team (CERT).

Hopefully, you will never have to prove yourself in a disaster emergency. However, if you do have to act in a time of crisis to save your family, your best defense is a good offense. Arm yourself with knowledge, and be ready to adapt, improvise, and overcome.

This guide is not designed to invoke fear or to generate a doomsday mindset. It is intended to educate and to inspire personal action. Hopefully, you will read this guide and stop to think about what you can do to be prepared for the worst-case scenario.

CHAPTER 1

Why Prepare?

There are real benefits to being prepared:

- Being prepared can reduce fear, anxiety, and losses that accompany disasters. Communities, families, and individuals should know what to do in the event of a fire and where to seek shelter during a tornado. They should be ready to evacuate their homes and take refuge in public shelters and know how to care for their basic medical needs.
- People can also reduce the impact of disasters (flood proofing, elevating a home or moving a home out of harm's way, and securing items that could shake loose in an earthquake) and sometimes avoid the danger completely.

The need to prepare is real:

- Disasters disrupt hundreds of thousands of lives every year. Each disaster has lasting effects, both to people and property.
- If a disaster occurs in your community, local government and disaster-relief organizations will try to help you, but you need to be ready as well. Local responders may not be able to reach you immediately, or they may need to focus their efforts elsewhere.
- You should know how to respond to severe weather or any disaster that could occur in your area—hurricanes, earthquakes, extreme cold, flooding, or terrorism.
- You should also be ready to be self-sufficient for at least three days. This may mean providing for your own shelter, first aid, food, water, and sanitation.

Using this guide makes preparation practical:

- This guide contains step-by-step advice on how to prepare for, respond to, and recover from disasters.

- Used in conjunction with information and instructions from local emergency management offices and the American Red Cross, this guide will give you what you need to be prepared.

USING THIS GUIDE TO PREPARE

The main reason to use this guide is to help protect yourself and your family in the event of an emergency. When you apply what you learn in this guide, you will be taking the necessary steps to be ready when an event occurs.

You have a responsibility to protect yourself and your family by knowing what to do before, during, and after an event. The following are some important steps that you should consider:

Before

- Know the risks and danger signs.
- Purchase insurance, including flood insurance (which is not part of your homeowner's policy).
- Develop plans for what to do.
- Assemble a disaster supplies kit.
- Volunteer to help others.

During

- Put your plan into action.
- Help others.
- Follow the advice and guidance of officials in charge.

After

- Attend to your family's medical, physical, and emotional needs.
- Repair damaged property.
- Take steps to prevent or reduce future loss.

This guide will teach you more about these steps and other actions that you should take to protect your family.

You should be prepared to seek out help from to others within your local community. Most emergencies are handled at the local government level, which puts a tremendous responsibility on the community for taking care of its citizens. Among the responsibilities faced by local officials are the following:

- Identifying hazards and assessing potential risk to the community.
- Enforcing building codes, zoning ordinances, and land-use management programs.
- Coordinating emergency plans to ensure a quick and effective response.

- Fighting fires and responding to hazardous materials incidents.
- Establishing warning systems.
- Stocking emergency supplies and equipment.
- Assessing damage and identifying needs.
- Evacuating the community to safer locations.
- Taking care of the injured.
- Sheltering those who cannot remain in their homes.
- Aiding recovery efforts.

If support and resources are needed beyond what the local level can provide, the community can request assistance from the state. The state may be able to provide supplemental resources such as money, equipment, and personnel to close the gap between what is needed and what is available at the local level. The state also coordinates the plans of the various jurisdictions so that activities do not interfere or conflict with each other. To ensure personnel know what to do and efforts are in agreement, the state may offer a program that provides jurisdictions the opportunity to train and exercise together.

Additionally, the federal government can provide resources to augment state and local efforts. These resources can be in the following form:

- Public educational materials, such as this guide, that can be used to prepare individuals for protecting themselves from hazards.
- Financial grants for equipment, training, exercises, personnel, and programs.
- Grants and loans to help communities respond to and recover from disasters so severe that the president of the United States has deemed them beyond state and local capabilities.
- Research findings that can help reduce losses from disaster.
- Technical assistance to help build stronger programs.

Start by reading, which will be the foundation of your disaster preparedness. Chapter 2 provides basic information that is common to all hazards and covers how to create and maintain an emergency plan and disaster supplies kit.

CHAPTER 2

Be Prepared: The Basics

In this chapter, you will learn preparedness strategies that are common to all disasters. You plan only once and are able to apply your plan to all types of hazards. The following material is covered in this chapter:

- Advice about what information you should obtain from the community to help form the foundation of your plan. You will need to find out about hazards that threaten the community, how the population will be warned, evacuation routes to be used in times of disaster, and the emergency plans of the community and others that will impact your plan.
- Guidance on specific content that you and your family will need to develop and include in your plan on how to escape from your residence, communicate with one another during times of disaster, shut off household utilities, insure against financial loss, acquire basic safety skills, address special needs such as disabilities, take care of animals, and seek shelter.
- Checklists of items to consider including in your disaster supplies kit that will meet your family's needs following a disaster, whether you are at home or at other locations.

The information provided in this chapter is critical to your family's preparedness. When you have read this material and you understand it completely, share your findings with each member of your family. When you complete this chapter, you will be able to do the following:

- Get informed about hazards and emergencies that may affect you and your family.
- Develop an emergency plan.
- Collect and assemble a disaster supplies kit.

- Learn where to seek shelter from all types of hazards.
- Identify the community warning systems and evacuation routes.
- Include in your plan required information from community and school plans.
- Learn what to do for specific hazards.
- Practice and maintain your plan.

DO YOUR HOMEWORK

Learn about the hazards that may strike your community, the risks that you face from these hazards, and your community's plans for warning and evacuation. You can obtain this information from your local emergency management office or your local chapter of the American Red Cross.

Hazards

Ask local authorities about each possible hazard or emergency, and note your findings and suggestions for reducing your family's risk.

You also can consult FEMA (www.fema.gov) for hazard maps for your area.

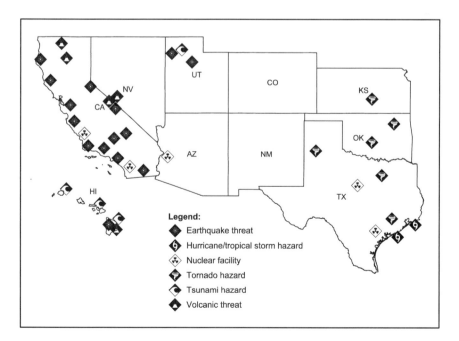

Figure 2.1: Disaster Threats in the Southwestern United States

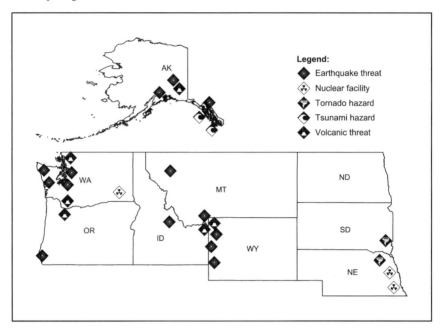

Figure 2.2: Disaster Threats in the Northwestern United States

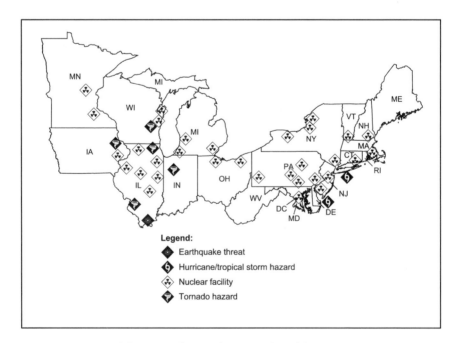

Figure 2.3: Disaster Threats in the Northeastern United States

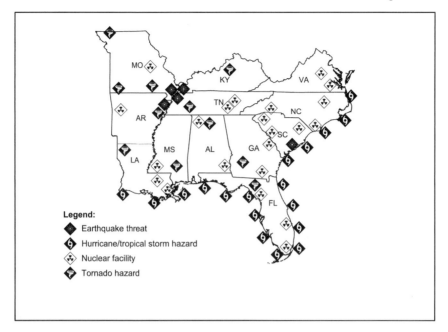

Figure 2.4: Disaster Threats in the Southeastern United States

Warning Systems and Signals

The Emergency Alert System (EAS) can address the entire nation on very short notice in case of a grave threat or national emergency. Ask if your local radio and TV stations participate in the EAS.

National Oceanic & Atmospheric Administration (NOAA) Weather Radio (NWR) is a nationwide network of radio stations broadcasting continuous weather information directly from a nearby National Weather Service (NWS) office to specially configured NOAA weather radio receivers. Determine if NOAA Weather Radio is available where you live. If so, consider purchasing a NOAA weather radio receiver.

Ask local authorities about methods used to warn your community. You should plan now for how you will react to an alert from each of the public warning systems used in your area. In the section below, fill in what you will do for each warning method.

Public Warning System — Your Family Action Plan?

- EAS:
- NOAA Weather:
- Telephone Trees:
- Community Sirens:

Table 2.1
Disaster Threats in Your Area

Potential emergency Risk:	High	Med.	Low	Mitigation plan
Flood	☐	☐	☐	
Hurricane	☐	☐	☐	
Thunderstorm	☐	☐	☐	
Tornado	☐	☐	☐	
Winter storm	☐	☐	☐	
Extreme heat	☐	☐	☐	
Earthquake	☐	☐	☐	
Volcano	☐	☐	☐	
Landslide/mudslide	☐	☐	☐	
Tsunami	☐	☐	☐	
Fire	☐	☐	☐	
Wildfire	☐	☐	☐	
Hazardous materials	☐	☐	☐	
Nuclear power plant	☐	☐	☐	
Explosion	☐	☐	☐	
Biological threat	☐	☐	☐	
Chemical threat	☐	☐	☐	
Nuclear blast	☐	☐	☐	
"Dirty" bomb/RDD	☐	☐	☐	
Pandemics	☐	☐	☐	
Other diseases	☐	☐	☐	

Evacuating Yourself and Your Family

When community evacuations become necessary, local officials provide information to the public through the media. In some circumstances, other warning methods, such as sirens or telephone calls, also are used. Additionally, there may be circumstances under which you and your family feel threatened or endangered and you need to leave your home, school, or the workplace to avoid these situations.

The amount of time you have to leave will depend on the hazard. If the event is a weather condition, such as a hurricane that can be monitored, you might have a day or two to get ready. However, many disasters allow no time for people to gather even the most basic necessities, which is why advanced planning is essential.

Ask local authorities about emergency evacuation routes. Evacuations are more common than many people realize. Hundreds of times each year, transportation and industrial accidents release harmful substances, forcing thousands of people to leave their homes. Fires and floods cause evacuations even more frequently. Almost every year, people along the Gulf and Atlantic coasts evacuate in the face of approaching hurricanes.

Evacuation Guidelines

- Write out evacuation route directions (turn by turn), and mark the route on a current map. Keep copies in your vehicle(s) and in your disaster supplies kit. Also consider planning multiple evacuation routes to use in the event of an emergency, and preprogram these routes into a GPS navigation tool.
- Keep a full tank of gas in your car if an evacuation seems likely. Gas stations may be closed during emergencies and unable to pump gas during power outages. Plan to take one car per family to reduce congestion and delay.
- Gather your disaster supplies kit.
- Make transportation arrangements with friends or your local government if you do not own a car.
- Wear sturdy shoes and clothing that provide some protection, such as long pants, a long-sleeved shirt, and a cap.
- Listen to a battery-powered radio, and follow local evacuation instructions.
- Secure your home as follows:
  - Close and lock doors and windows.
  - Unplug electrical equipment, such as radios and televisions, and small appliances, such as toasters and microwaves.
  - Leave freezers and refrigerators plugged in, unless there is a risk of flooding.
- Gather your family and go if you are instructed to evacuate immediately.
- Let others know where you are going.
- Leave early enough to avoid being trapped by severe weather.
- Follow recommended evacuation routes. Do not take shortcuts; they may be blocked.
- Be alert for washed-out roads and bridges.
- Do not drive into flooded areas.
- Stay away from downed power lines.

Community and Other Plans

Ask local officials direct questions about your community's disaster/emergency plans. For example:

Does my community have a plan?
Can I obtain a copy?
What does the plan contain?
How often is it updated?
What should I know about the plan?
What hazards does it cover?

In addition to finding out about your community's plan, it is important that you know what plans are in place for your workplace and your children's school or day-care center.

1. Ask your employer about workplace policies regarding disasters and emergencies, including understanding how you will be provided emergency and warning information.

2. Contact your children's school or day-care center to discuss their disaster procedures.

School Emergency Plans

Know your children's school emergency plan:

- Ask how the school will communicate with families during a crisis.
- Ask if the school stores adequate food, water, and other basic supplies.
- Find out if the school is prepared to shelter in place if need be and where they plan to go if they must get away.

In cases where schools institute procedures to shelter in place, you may not be permitted to drive to the school to pick up your children. Even if you go to the school, the doors will likely be locked to keep your children safe. Monitor local media outlets for announcements about changes in school openings and closings, and follow the directions of local emergency officials.

For more information on developing emergency preparedness plans for schools, visit the U.S. Department of Education on the Web at http://www.ed.gov/emergencyplan. Talk with your children and inform them about what to expect in the event of an emergency while they are at school.

Workplace Plans

If you are an employer, make sure your workplace has a building evacuation plan that is regularly practiced.

- Take a critical look at your heating, ventilation, and air-conditioning system to determine if it is secure or if it could feasibly be upgraded to better filter potential contaminants, and be sure you know how to turn it off if you need to.
- Think about what to do if your employees can't go home.
- Make sure you have appropriate supplies on hand.

EMERGENCY PLANNING AND CHECKLISTS

Now that you've learned about what can happen and how your community is prepared to respond to emergencies, prepare your family by creating a family disaster plan. You can begin this process by gathering family members and reviewing the information you obtained in the previous section (hazards, warning systems, evacuation routes, and community and other plans). Discuss with them what you would do if family members are not home when a warning is issued. Additionally, your family plan should address the following items:

- Escape routes
- Family communications
- Utility shutoff and safety
- Insurance and vital records
- Special needs
- Caring for animals
- Safety skills

Escape Routes

Draw a floor plan of your home. Use a blank sheet of paper for each floor. Mark two escape routes from each room. Make sure children understand the drawings. Post a copy of the drawings at eye level in each child's room. Establish a place for your family to meet in the event of an emergency. In the section below, fill in where you will meet for each proximity.

Proximity to Home—Your Family Meeting Place?

- Nearby Home:
- Outside Neighborhood:

Family Communications

Your family may not be together when disaster strikes, so plan how you will contact each other. Think about how you will communicate in different situations.

Complete a contact card for each family member. Have family members keep these cards handy in a wallet, purse, or backpack. You may want to send one to school with each child to keep on file. Pick a friend or relative who lives out of state for household members to notify when they are safe.

You can find sample contact cards in the appendix. Post copies of all this information in a location readily accessible to all family members. Also include copies in your family disaster supplies kit.

Utility Shutoff and Safety

In the event of a disaster, local authorities may instruct you to shut off the utility service at your home. You should know how to shut off natural gas, water, and electricity.

Preparing to Shut Off Natural Gas

Natural gas leaks and explosions are responsible for a significant number of fires following disasters. It is vital that all household members know how to shut off natural gas.

Contact your local gas company for guidance on preparation and response regarding gas appliances and gas service to your home because there are different gas shutoff procedures for different gas meter configurations.

When you learn the proper shutoff procedure for your meter, share the information with everyone in your household. Be sure not to turn off the gas when practicing the proper gas shutoff procedure.

If you smell gas or hear a blowing or hissing noise, open a window and get everyone out quickly. Turn off the gas, using the outside main valve if you can, and call the gas company from a neighbor's home.

> **CAUTION:** If you turn off the gas for any reason, a qualified professional must turn it back on. *Never* attempt to turn the gas back on yourself.

Preparing to Shut Off Water

Water quickly becomes a precious resource following many disasters. It is vital that all household members learn how to shut off the water at the main house valve.

- Cracked lines may pollute the water supply to your house. It is wise to shut off your water until you hear from authorities that it is safe for drinking.
- The effects of gravity may drain the water in your hot water heater and toilet tanks unless you trap it in your house by shutting off the main house valve (not the street valve in the cement box at the curb—this valve is extremely difficult to turn and requires a special tool).
- Locate the shutoff valve for the water line that enters your house (contact the water company if you are unsure about what to look for).
- Make sure this valve can be completely shut off. Your valve may be rusted open, or it may only partially close. Replace it if necessary.
- Label this valve with a tag for easy identification, and make sure all household members know where it is located.

Preparing to Shut Off Electricity

Electrical sparks have the potential of igniting natural gas if it is leaking. It is wise to teach all responsible household members where and how to shut off the electricity.

- Locate your electricity circuit box.
- Teach all responsible household members how to shut off the electricity to the entire house.

> **FOR YOUR SAFETY:** Always shut off all the individual circuits before shutting off the main circuit breaker.

Insurance and Vital Records

Obtain property, health, and life insurance if you do not have them. Review existing policies for the amount and extent of coverage to ensure that what you have in place is what is required for you and your family for all possible hazards.

If you live in a flood-prone area, consider purchasing flood insurance to reduce your risk of flood loss. Buying flood insurance to cover the value of a building and its contents will not only provide greater peace of mind, but will speed the recovery if a flood occurs.

Inventory home possessions, and make a record of your personal property for insurance purposes. Take photos or a video of the interior and exterior of your home. Include personal belongings in your inventory.

You should store important documents (including insurance policies, deeds, property records, and other important papers) in a safe place. Consider securing a safety deposit box located away from your home. Make copies of important documents for your disaster supplies kit.

Consider saving money in an emergency savings account that could be used in any crisis. It is advisable to keep a small amount of cash or traveler's checks at home in a safe place where you can quickly access them in case of evacuation.

Special Needs

If you or someone close to you has a disability or a special need, you may have to take additional steps to protect yourself and your family in an emergency. For example:

- **Hearing Impaired**—May need to make special arrangements to receive warnings.
- **Mobility Impaired**—May need special assistance to get to a shelter.
- **Single Working Parent**—May need help to plan for children in the event of a disaster or emergency.
- **Non-English Speakers**—May need assistance planning for and responding to emergencies (community and cultural groups may be able to help keep people informed).
- **Nondrivers** —May need to make arrangements for transportation.
- **Special Dietary Needs**—Take precautions to have an adequate emergency food supply.

If you have special needs, follow these guidelines:

- Find out about special assistance that may be available in your community. Register with the office of emergency services or the local fire department for assistance so needed help can be provided.
- Create a network of neighbors, relatives, friends, and coworkers to aid you in an emergency. Discuss your needs and make sure everyone knows how to operate necessary equipment.
- Discuss your needs with your employer.

- If you are mobility impaired and live or work in a high-rise building, have an escape chair.
- If you live in an apartment building, ask the management to mark accessible exits clearly and to make arrangements to help you leave the building.
- Keep specialized items ready, including extra wheelchair batteries, oxygen, catheters, medication, food for service animals, and any other items you might need.
- Be sure to make provisions for medications that require refrigeration.
- Keep a list of the type and model numbers of the medical devices you require.

Caring for Animals

Animals also are affected by disasters. To prepare a plan for caring for pets and large animals, do the following:

- Identify shelter.
- Gather pet supplies.
- Ensure that your pet has proper identification tags and up-to-date veterinarian records.
- Provide a pet carrier and leash.

Prepare to shelter your pet as follows:

- Call your local emergency management office, animal shelter, or animal control office to get advice and information.
- Keep veterinary records to prove vaccinations are current.
- Find out which local hotels and motels allow pets and where pet boarding facilities are located. Be sure to research some outside your local area in case local facilities close.
- Know that, with the exception of service animals, pets are not typically permitted in emergency shelters as they may affect the health and safety of other occupants.

If you have large animals such as horses, cattle, sheep, goats, or pigs on your property, take the following steps:

- Ensure that all animals have some form of identification.
- Evacuate animals whenever possible. Map out primary and secondary routes in advance.
- Make available vehicles and trailers needed for transporting and supporting each type of animal. Also make available experienced handlers and drivers.

NOTE: It is best to allow animals a chance to become accustomed to vehicular travel so they are less frightened and easier to move.

- Ensure destinations have food, water, veterinary care, and handling equipment.
- If evacuation is not possible, animal owners must decide whether to move large animals to shelter or turn them outside.

Safety Skills

It is important that family members know how to administer first aid and CPR, and how to use a fire extinguisher.

Learn First Aid and CPR

Take a first-aid and CPR class. Local American Red Cross chapters can provide information about this type of training. Official certification by the American Red Cross provides, under the so-called good Samaritan law, protection for those giving first aid. Many employers will voluntarily arrange these classes for personnel at no charge.

Learn How to Use a Fire Extinguisher

Be sure everyone in your family knows how to use your fire extinguisher(s) as well as where it is kept. You should have, at a minimum, an ABC type. Contact your local fire department to arrange a safety demonstration.

ASSEMBLE A DISASTER SUPPLIES KIT

You may need to survive on your own after a disaster. This means having your own food, water, and other supplies in sufficient quantity to last for at least three days (one gallon, or about four liters, of water per person, per day). Local officials and relief workers will be on the scene after a disaster, but they cannot reach everyone immediately. You could get help in hours, or it might take days.

Basic services such as electricity, gas, water, sewage treatment, and telephones may be cut off for days, or even a week or longer. Or, you may have to evacuate at a moment's notice and take essentials with you. You probably will not have the opportunity to shop or search for the supplies you need. A disaster supplies kit is a collection of basic items that members of a household may need in the event of a disaster.

Kit Locations

Since you do not know where you will be when an emergency occurs, prepare supplies for home, work, and vehicles.

Your disaster supplies kit should contain essential food, water, and supplies for at least three days. Keep this kit in a designated place, and have it ready in case you have to leave your home quickly. Make sure all family members know where the kit is kept. Additionally, you may want to consider having supplies for sheltering for up to two weeks. This kit should be in one container and ready to "grab and go" in case you are evacuated from your workplace. Make sure you have food and water in the kit. Also, be sure to have comfortable walking shoes at your workplace in case an evacuation requires you to walk long distances.

In case you are stranded, keep a kit of emergency supplies in your car. This kit should contain food, water, first-aid supplies, flares, jumper cables, and seasonal supplies.

Water

How much water do you need? You should store at least one gallon, or about four liters, of water per person per day. A normally active person needs at least one-half gallon, or about two liters, of water daily just for drinking. Additionally, in determining adequate quantities, consider the following factors:

- Individual needs vary, depending on age, physical condition, activity, diet, and climate.
- Children, nursing mothers, and ill people need more water.
- Very hot temperatures can double the amount of water needed.
- A medical emergency might require additional water.

How should you store water? To prepare a safe and reliable emergency supply of water, purchase commercially bottled water. Keep bottled water in its original container, and do not open it until you need to use it. Observe the expiration or "use by" date.

If you are preparing your own containers of water, purchase food-grade water storage containers from surplus or camping supplies stores to use for water storage. Before filling with water, thoroughly clean the containers with dishwashing soap and water, and rinse completely so there is no residual soap.

If you choose to use your own storage containers, choose two-liter plastic soft drink bottles—not plastic jugs or cardboard containers that have had milk or fruit juice in them. Milk protein and fruit sugars cannot be adequately removed from these containers and provide an environment for bacterial growth when water is stored in them. Cardboard containers also leak easily and are not designed for long-term storage of liquids. Also, do not use glass containers, because they can break and they are heavy.

If storing water in plastic soda bottles, follow these steps:

- Thoroughly clean the bottles with dishwashing soap and water, and rinse completely so there is no residual soap.
- Sanitize the bottles by adding a solution of 1 teaspoon, or about 5ml, of unscented liquid household chlorine bleach to a quart, or about a liter, of water. Swish the sanitizing solution in the bottle so that it touches all surfaces.
- After sanitizing the bottle, thoroughly rinse out the sanitizing solution with clean water.

- Fill the bottle to the top with regular tap water. If the tap water has been commercially treated from a water utility with chlorine, you do not need to add anything else to the water to keep it clean.
- If the water you are using comes from a well or water source that is not treated with chlorine, add two drops of unscented liquid household chlorine bleach to the water.
- Tightly close the container using the original cap. Be careful not to contaminate the cap by touching the inside of it with your finger.
- Place a date on the outside of the container indicating when you filled it.
- Store in a cool, dark place.
- Replace the water every six months if not using commercially bottled water.

Food

When you assemble your food supplies, consider these factors:

- Avoid foods that will make you thirsty. Choose salt-free crackers, whole grain cereals, and canned foods with high liquid content.
- Stock canned foods, dry mixes, and other staples that do not require refrigeration, cooking, water, or special preparation. You may already have many of these on hand.

NOTE: Be sure to include a manual can opener.

- Include special dietary needs.

Basic Disaster Supplies Kit

Recommendations:

- Three-day supply of nonperishable food.
- Three-day supply of water—one gallon, or about four liters, of water per person, per day.
- Portable, battery-powered radio or television and extra batteries.
- Flashlight and extra batteries.
- First-aid kit, first-aid manual, and this guide.
- Sanitation and hygiene items (moist towelettes and toilet paper).
- Matches and waterproof container.
- Whistle.
- Extra clothing.
- Kitchen accessories and cooking utensils, including a can opener.
- Photocopies of credit and identification cards.
- Cash and coins.

- Special needs items, such as prescription medications, eyeglasses, contact lens solutions, and hearing-aid batteries.
- Items for infants, such as formula, diapers, bottles, and pacifiers.
- Other items to meet your unique family needs.

If you live in a cold climate, you must think about warmth. It is possible that you will not have heat. Think about your clothing and bedding supplies. Be sure to include one complete change of clothing and shoes per person, including the following items:

- Jacket or coat
- Long pants
- Long-sleeve shirt
- Sturdy shoes
- Hat, mittens, and scarf
- Sleeping bag or warm blanket (per person)

Be sure to account for growing children and other family changes. See the Appendix for a detailed checklist of disaster supplies. You may want to add some of the items listed to your basic disaster supplies kit, depending on the specific needs of your family.

Maintaining Your Disaster Supplies Kit

Just as important as putting your supplies together is maintaining them so they are safe to use when needed. Here are some tips to keep your supplies ready and in good condition:

- Keep canned foods in a dry place where the temperature is cool.
- Store boxed food in tightly closed plastic or metal containers to protect from pests and to extend its shelf life.
- Throw out any canned good that becomes swollen, dented, or corroded.
- Use foods before they go bad, and replace them with fresh supplies.
- Place new items at the back of the storage area and older ones in the front.
- Change stored food and water supplies every six months. Be sure to write the date you store it on all containers.
- Rethink your needs every year, and update your kit as your family needs change (Do this when you change the batteries in your smoke detectors each year.)
- Keep items in airtight plastic bags, and put your entire disaster supplies kit in one or two easy-to-carry containers, such as an unused trash can, camping backpack, or duffel bag.

SHELTER

Taking shelter is critical in times of disaster. Sheltering is appropriate when conditions require that you seek protection in your home, place of employment, or other location where you are when disaster strikes. Sheltering outside the hazard area would include staying with friends and relatives, seeking commercial lodging, or staying in a mass-care facility operated by disaster relief groups in conjunction with local authorities.

To effectively shelter, you must first consider the hazard and then choose a place in your home or other building that is safe for that hazard. For example, for a tornado, a room should be selected that is in a basement or an interior room on the lowest level away from corners, windows, doors, and outside walls. Because the safest locations to seek shelter vary by hazard, sheltering is discussed in the various hazard sections. These discussions include recommendations for sealing the shelter if the hazard warrants this type of protection.

Even though mass-care shelters often provide water, food, medicine, and basic sanitary facilities, you should plan to take your disaster supplies kit with you so you will have the supplies you require. Mass-care sheltering can involve living with many people in a confined space, which can be difficult and unpleasant. To avoid conflicts in this stressful situation, it is important to cooperate with shelter managers and others assisting them. Keep in mind that alcoholic beverages and weapons are forbidden in emergency shelters and that smoking is restricted.

The length of time you are required to shelter may be short, such as during a tornado warning, or long, such as during a winter storm. It is important that you stay in shelter until local authorities say it is safe to leave. Additionally, you should take turns listening to radio broadcasts and maintain a 24-hour safety watch.

During extended periods of sheltering, you will need to manage water and food supplies to ensure that you and your family have the required supplies and quantities. Guidance on how to accomplish this follows.

Managing Water

- Allow people to drink according to their needs. Many people need even more than the average of one-half gallon, or about two liters, per day. The individual amount needed depends on age, physical activity, physical condition, and time of year.

- Never ration water unless ordered to do so by authorities. Drink the amount you need today, and try to find more for tomorrow. Under no circumstances should a person drink less than one quart (four cups), or about one liter, of water each day. You can minimize the amount of water your body needs by reducing activity and staying cool.

- Drink water that you know is not contaminated first. If necessary, suspicious water, such as cloudy water from regular faucets or water from streams or ponds, can be used after it has been treated. If water treatment is not possible, put off drinking suspicious water as long as possible, but do not become dehydrated.

- Do not drink carbonated beverages instead of drinking water. Carbonated beverages do not meet drinking-water requirements. Caffeinated drinks and alcohol dehydrate the body, which increases the need for drinking water.
- Turn off the main water valves. You will need to protect the water sources already in your home from contamination if you hear reports of broken water or sewage lines, or if local officials advise you of a problem. To close the incoming water source, locate the incoming valve and turn it to the closed position. Be sure you and other family members know how to perform this important procedure.
- To use the water in your pipes, let air into the plumbing by turning on the faucet in your home at the highest level. A small amount of water will trickle out. Then obtain water from the lowest faucet in the home.
- To use the water in your hot-water tank, be sure the electricity or gas is off, and open the drain at the bottom of the tank. Start the water flowing by turning off the water intake valve at the tank and turning on the hot water faucet. Refill the tank before turning the gas or electricity back on. If the gas is turned off, a professional will be needed to turn it back on.

Safe Water Sources

- Melt ice cubes.
- Drain water from the water heater (if the unit is undamaged).
- Reclaim liquids from canned goods, including fruit and vegetable juices.
- Drain water from plumbing water supply pipes (*not* waste plumbing).
- Collect water using a solar still.

Dangerous Water Sources

- *Do not* drink water from radiators.
- *Do not* drink water from home heating system boiler.
- *Do not* drink water from water beds.
- *Do not* drink water from the toilet bowl or flush tank.
- *Do not* drink water from swimming pools and spas (however, you can use water from these sources for personal hygiene and cleaning).

Treat all water of uncertain quality before using it for drinking, food washing or preparation, washing dishes, brushing teeth, or making ice. In addition to having a bad odor and taste, contaminated water can contain microorganisms (germs) that cause diseases such as dysentery, cholera, typhoid, and hepatitis.

There are many ways to treat water. None is perfect. Often the best solution is a combination of methods. Before treating water, let any suspended particles settle to the bottom, or strain them through coffee filters or layers of clean cloth. Make sure you have the necessary materials in your disaster supplies kit for the chosen water treatment method.

There are three water treatment methods:

- Boiling
- Chlorination
- Distillation

These instructions are for treating water of uncertain quality in an emergency situation, when no other reliable clean water source is available, or you have used all of your stored water.

Boiling

Boiling is the safest method of treating water. In a large pot or kettle, bring water to a rolling boil for 1 full minute, keeping in mind that some water will evaporate. Let the water cool before drinking.

Boiled water will taste better if you put oxygen back into it by pouring the water back and forth between two clean containers. This also will improve the taste of stored water.

Chlorination

You can use household liquid bleach to kill microorganisms. Use only regular household liquid bleach that contains 5.25 to 6.0 percent sodium hypochlorite. Do not use scented bleaches, color safe bleaches, or bleaches with added cleaners. Because the potency of bleach diminishes with time, use bleach from a newly opened or unopened bottle.

Add about 16 drops (1/8 teaspoon, or about 1ml) of bleach per gallon of water, stir, and let stand for 30 minutes. The water should have a slight bleach odor. If it doesn't, then repeat the dosage, and let stand another 15 minutes. If it still does not smell of chlorine, discard it and find another source of water.

Other chemicals, such as iodine or water treatment products sold in camping or surplus stores that do not contain 5.25 to 6.0 percent sodium hypochlorite as the only active ingredient are not recommended and should not be used.

Distillation

While the two methods described above will kill most microbes in water, distillation will remove microbes (germs) that resist these methods, as well as heavy metals, salts, and most other chemicals.

Distillation involves boiling water and then collecting only the vapor that condenses. The condensed vapor will not include salt or most other impurities. To distill, fill a pot halfway with water. Tie a cup to the handle on the pot's lid so that the cup will hang right side up when the lid is upside down (make sure the cup is not dangling into the water) and boil the water for 20 minutes. The water that drips from the lid into the cup is distilled.

All three water treatment methods kill microbes, but only distillation removes other contaminants (heavy metals, salts, and most other chemicals). Distillation is the preferred water treatment method.

Managing Food Supplies

Safe Food Practices

- Keep food in covered containers.
- Keep cooking and eating utensils clean.
- Keep garbage in closed containers outside (bury garbage if necessary).
- Keep your hands clean by washing them frequently with soap and water that has been boiled or disinfected.
- Use only preprepared canned baby formula for infants.
- Discard any food that has come into contact with contaminated floodwater.
- Discard any food that has been at room temperature for two hours or more.
- Discard any food that has an unusual odor, color, or texture.

Dangerous Food Practices

- Do not eat foods from cans that are swollen, dented, or corroded, even though the product may look safe to eat.
- Do not eat any food that looks or smells abnormal, even if the can looks normal.
- Do not use powdered formulas with untreated water.
- Do not let garbage accumulate inside, for fire and sanitation reasons.

NOTE: Thawed food usually can be eaten if it is still refrigerator cold. It can be refrozen if it still contains ice crystals. To be safe, remember, "When in doubt, throw it out."

Cooking

- Alternative cooking sources in times of emergency include candle warmers, chafing dishes, fondue pots, or a fireplace.
- Charcoal grills and camp stoves are for outdoor use only.
- Commercially canned food may be eaten out of the can without warming.
- To heat food in a can, follow these steps:
  1. Remove the label.
  2. Thoroughly wash and disinfect the can. (Use a diluted solution of 1 part bleach to 10 parts water.)
  3. Open the can before heating.

Managing without Power

Here are two options for keeping food safe if you are without power for a long period:

- Look for alternate storage space for your perishable food.
- Use dry ice. Twenty-five pounds, or about 11kg, of dry ice will keep a 10-cubic-foot, or 3-cubic meter, freezer below freezing for three to four days. Use care when handling dry ice, and wear dry, heavy gloves to avoid injury.

HAZARD-SPECIFIC PREPAREDNESS

There are actions that should be taken before, during, and after an event that are unique to each hazard. For example:

- Seeking a safe shelter during a tornado.
- Reducing property loss from a hurricane.

OTHER CONSIDERATIONS IN THE WAKE OF A DISASTER

Volunteer-Responder Convergence

Convergence is the spontaneous influx of people, goods, and services into a disaster zone. Convergence may be helpful and even needed, but it can also cause overwhelming problems including the following:

- Confusion
- Traffic congestion (both people and vehicles)
- Compromised security
- Personnel accountability
- Wasted critical resources
- Delayed lifesaving aid

The intense media attention and the emotional impact of a disaster on the general public can generate amplified conditions that turn convergence into a problem. If you are not a trained emergency responder, resist the impulse to immediately go to the scene. Consider volunteering money or relief supplies instead. Think carefully about how you can best assist the victims, and then act. If you do go to the scene after a reasonable amount of time has passed to allow authorities to organize, seek out representatives from a recognized relief agency (for example, the American Red Cross) for direction. You will likely be most effective as part of a larger, well-organized team.

Strategic emergency planning, by organizations that appreciate the necessity for improvisation and adaptability, is vital to an effective disaster response. Get involved in your community, and consider completing an American Red Cross First Aid or CPR course, or Community Emergency Response Team (CERT) course.

Peripheral Hazards

Be aware of new safety issues created by the disaster. Watch for washed-out roads, contaminated buildings, contaminated water, gas leaks, broken glass, damaged electrical wiring/downed power lines, and slippery floors.

Carefully consider the safety risks before attempting extensive home repairs yourself. Many people become victims after a disaster because they attempt repairs (like roofing or electrical work) by themselves right after an event.

Hopefully, you had time to shut off gas at the meter before a disaster. Find a qualified professional to safely turn the gas back on.

Disasters and life-threatening situations will exacerbate the unpredictable nature of wild animals (an even cause domestic animals to act unexpectedly). Do not approach animals that have taken refuge in your home. Watch your pets closely, and keep them leashed for several days after a disaster. Inform local authorities about health and safety issues, including chemical spills, downed power lines, washed-out roads, smoldering insulation, and dead animals.

Generator Safety

Take precautions when using a generator in the event of an emergency:

- Select a generator that is listed with the Underwriter's Laboratory (UL) or Factory Mutual (FM).
- Choose a generator that produces more power than will be drawn by the combination of lighting, appliances, and equipment you plan to connect.
- Carefully follow the manufacturer's directions.
- Let the generator cool down before refueling.
- Connect the equipment you want to power directly to the outlets on the generator but *do not* hook up a generator to your home's electrical service.
- Operate the generator in a well-ventilated area away from your personal living space to avoid the dangers of carbon monoxide poisoning.

PRACTICING AND MAINTAINING YOUR PLAN

Once you have developed your plan, you need to practice and maintain it. For example, ask questions to make sure your family remembers meeting places, phone numbers, and safety rules. Conduct drills, such as drop, cover, and hold on for earthquakes. Test fire alarms. Replace and update disaster supplies regularly.

CHAPTER 3

Resources for More Information

INTERNATIONAL

- American National Red Cross®: http://www.redcross.org
- United Nations Scientific Committee on the Effects of Atomic Radiation (UNSCEAR): http://www.unscear.org
- World Health Organization (WHO), the United Nations specialized agency for health: http://www.who.int

U.S. FEDERAL GOVERNMENT

- Agency for Toxic Substances and Disease Registry (ATSDR): http://www.atsdr.cdc.gov
- Center for Mental Health Services: http://mentalhealth.samhsa.gov
- Centers for Disease Control and Prevention (CDC): Toll-Free Telephone Hotline (800) 232–4636; http://www.cdc.gov
- Citizen Corps (coordinates community emergency preparedness volunteer activities): http://www.citizencorps.gov
- Code of Federal Regulations (CFR): http://www.gpoaccess.gov/cfr
- Environmental Protection Agency (EPA): http://www.epa.gov
- Federal Bureau of Investigation: http://www.fbi.gov
- Federal Communications Commission (FCC): http://www.fcc.gov
- Federal Emergency Management Agency (FEMA): http://www.fema.gov
- Federal Geographic Data Committee (FGDC) Homeland Security Working Group Symbology Reference: http://www.fgdc.gov/HSWG

- Federal Trade Commission (FTC) consumer information (including information about identity theft): http://www.ftc.gov/ftc/consumer.htm
- National Atlas of the United States® by the U.S. Department of the Interior (nationalatlas.gov™): http://www.nationalatlas.gov
- National Center for Post Traumatic Stress Disorder: http://www.ncptsd.va.gov
- National Disaster Medical System: http://ndms.dhhs.gov
- National Institute for Occupational Safety and Health (NIOSH): http://www.cdc.gov/niosh/homepage.html
- National Institute of Mental Health: http://www.nimh.nih.gov
- National Interagency Fire Center: http://www.nifc.gov
- National Oceanic and Atmospheric Administration's (NOAA) National Weather Service (NWS): http://www.nws.noaa.gov
- National Poison Center Toll-Free Telephone Hotline: (800) 222–1222
- Occupational Safety & Health Administration (OSHA): http://www.osha.gov
- PandemicFlu.gov (managed by the Department of Health and Human Services, one-stop access to U.S. government avian and pandemic flu information): http://www.pandemicflu.gov
- Ready campaign is part of the U.S. Department of Homeland Security's national public service advertising campaign designed to help Americans prepare for and respond to disasters and emergencies (also includes links to information designed specifically for children): http://www.ready.gov
- U.S. Army Edgewood Chemical Biological Center (ECBC): http://www.ecbc.army.mil
- U.S. Department of Agriculture: http://www.usda.gov
- U.S. Department of Education information on developing emergency preparedness plans for schools: http://www.ed.gov/emergencyplan
- U.S. Department of Homeland Security (DHS): http://www.dhs.gov
- U.S. Department of State: http://www.state.gov
- U.S. Food and Drug Administration (FDA): http://www.fda.gov
- U.S. Geological Survey provides information to help minimize loss of life and property from natural disasters: http://www.usgs.gov
- U.S. Secret Service: http://www.secretservice.gov

STATE AND LOCAL AUTHORITIES

- Alabama: http://www.ema.alabama.gov
- Alaska: http://www.ak-prepared.com
- Arizona: http://www.dem.state.az.us
- Arkansas: http://www.adem.state.ar.us
- California: http://www.oes.ca.gov
- Colorado: http://www.dola.state.co.us/oem
- Connecticut: http://www.ct.gov/demhs

- Delaware: http://www.state.de.us/dema
- Florida: http://www.floridadisaster.org
- Georgia: http://www.gema.state.ga.us
- Hawaii: http://www.scd.hawaii.gov
- Idaho: http://www.bhs.idaho.gov
- Illinois: http://www.state.il.us/iema
- Indiana: http://www.in.gov/dhs
- Iowa: http://www.iowahomelandsecurity.org
- Kansas: http://www.accesskansas.org/kdem
- Kentucky: http://kyem.ky.gov
- Louisiana: http://www.loep.state.la.us
- Maine: http://www.state.me.us/mema
- Maryland: http://www.mema.state.md.us
- Massachusetts: http://www.state.ma.us/mema
- Michigan: http://www.michigan.gov/som/0,1607,7-192-29941—-,00.html
- Minnesota: http://www.hsem.state.mn.us
- Mississippi: http://www.msema.org
- Missouri: http://sema.dps.mo.gov
- Montana: http://dma.mt.gov/des
- Nebraska: http://www.nema.ne.gov
- Nevada: http://dem.state.nv.us
- New Hampshire: http://www.nh.gov/safety
- New Jersey: http://www.state.nj.us/njoem
- New Mexico: http://www.dps.nm.org/emergency
- New York: http://www.semo.state.ny.us
- North Carolina: http://www.dem.dcc.state.nc.us
- North Dakota: http://www.nd.gov/des
- Ohio: http://ema.ohio.gov
- Oklahoma: http://www.ok.gov/OEM
- Oregon: http://egov.oregon.gov/OOHS/OEM
- Pennsylvania: http://www.pema.state.pa.us
- Rhode Island: http://www.riema.ri.gov
- South Carolina: http://www.scemd.org
- South Dakota: http://oem.sd.gov
- Tennessee: http://www.tnema.org
- Texas: http://www.txdps.state.tx.us/dem
- Utah: http://dhls.utah.gov
- Vermont: http://www.dps.state.vt.us/vem

- Virginia: http://www.vdem.state.va.us
- Washington, D.C.: http://dcema.dc.gov
- Washington State: http://emd.wa.gov
- West Virginia: http://www.wvdhsem.gov
- Wisconsin: http://emergencymanagement.wi.gov
- Wyoming: http://wyohomelandsecurity.state.wy.us

COMMERCIAL AND OTHERS

- Amateur Radio Emergency Service (ARES®) provides emergency communications: http://www.ares.org
- Ambu® diagnostic and life-supporting equipment and solutions: http://www.ambuusa.com
- American Conference of Governmental Industrial Hygienists (ACGIH®): http://acgih.org
- American Humane Association®: http://www.americanhumane.org
- American Industrial Hygiene Association (AIHA®): http://www.aiha.org
- American National Standards Institute (ANSI®): http://www.ansi.org
- American Psychological Association (APA®) information about dealing with disasters: http://www.apa.org/topics/topicdisasters.html
- American Society for the Prevention of Cruelty to Animals (ASPCA®): http://www.aspca.org
- American Veterinary Medical Association (AVMA®): http://www.avma.org
- AmeriGlo® safety lighting: http://www.ameriglo.net
- Anbex Inc. is a manufacturer and distributor of Potassium Iodide (KI) Tablets under the brand name IOSAT™: www.anbex.com
- AnnualCreditReport.com® is the official site established to help consumers to obtain their free annual credit report: (877) 322–8228; http://www.annualcreditreport.com
- Aqua Blox® Inc.: http://www.aquablox.com
- Cobra® Electronics Corp.: http://www.cobra.com
- Coghlan's outdoor products: http://www.coghlans.com
- Draeger Safety®: http://www.draeger.com
- Eton® Corp.: http://www.etoncorp.com
- Fire Fyter™ safes: http://www.firefyter.com
- FireKing® Security Group safes: http://www.fireking.com
- First Alert® home safety products: http://www.firstalert.com
- Franklin Mfg. Saf-Escape Ladder™: http://www.franklinmfg.com
- Garmin™ Ltd. GPS solutions: http://www.garmin.com
- General Ecology® Inc. water purification: http://www.generalecology.com

- Gerber® Legendary Blades™ knives and tools: http://www.gerbergear.com
- Germ-X® hand sanitizer: http://www.germx.com
- Honeywell® IFD™ high-performance air purifier: www.kaz.com
- Humane Society of the United States®: http://www.hsus.org
- Innotech Products Ltd.: www.heatermeals.com
- Kidde® fire extingusishers: http://www.kidde.com
- Kriana Corp. Krill® electronic light sticks: www.kriana.com
- Leatherman® multitools: http://www.leatherman.com
- LIFE Corp.® CPR mask: http://www.lifecorporation.com
- Lowrance® Electronics Inc.: http://www.lowrance.com
- Mine Safety Appliances Company (MSA®): http://www.msanorthamerica.com
- Motorola®: http://www.motorola.com
- MPI Outdoors Space® brand emergency blankets: http://www.mpioutdoors.com
- National Center for Missing & Exploited Children: http://www.missingkids.com
- National Child Traumatic Stress Network (NCTSN®): http://www.nctsn.org
- National Fire Protection Organization (NFPA®): http://www.nfpa.org
- National Memorial Institute for the Prevention of Terrorism (MIPT®): http://www.mipt.org
- North® Safety Products: http://www.northsafety.com
- OMRON® Healthcare Inc. digital ear thermometers: http://www.omronhealthcare.com
- OnDuty™ Inc. 4 in 1 Emergency Tool™: http://www.onduty1.com
- OptOutPrescreen.com® is the official site established to help consumers "Opt-Out" (or "Opt-In") of firm offers of credit or insurance: (888) 567–8688; http://www.optoutprescreen.com
- Pelican™ Products watertight cases: http://www.pelican.com
- PowerFlare® Corp.: http://www.pfdistributioncenter.com
- Radio Amateur Civil Emergency Service (RACES®): http://www.races.net
- Rand McNally® & Company atlas: http://www.randmcnally.com
- Ritchie® Navigation: http://www.ritchienavigation.com
- Sentry® Safe: http://www.sentrysafe.com
- Sima® Products Corp.: http://www.simaproducts.com
- SKB® Cases Corp.: http://www.skbcases.com
- SKYWARN® is a cooperative effort between the National Weather Service and communities: http://www.skywarn.org
- SOG®: http://www.sogknives.com
- STORM® Safety Whistles: http://www.stormwhistles.com
- SUUNTO® Oy: http://www.suunto.com
- 3M®: http://www.3m.com

- TOOLLOGIC® Inc.: http://www.toollogic.com
- TurboFlare 360™: http://www.turboflare360.com
- Water-Jel® Technologies first-aid products: http://www.waterjel.com
- Wikipedia® is a free, open-content, community-built online encyclopedia: http://www.wikipedia.org
- Wisconsin Pharmacal Company LLC Potable Aqua® Chlorine Dioxide water purification tablets: http://www.potableaqua.com
- The Wornick™ Company EverSafe™ emergency meal kits: http://www.getever safe.com
- Zee® Medical Inc.: http://zeemedical.com

CHAPTER 4

Natural Hazards

This chapter includes information about many types of natural hazards. Natural hazards are natural events that threaten lives, property, and other assets. Often, natural hazards can be predicted. They tend to occur repeatedly in the same geographical locations because they are related to weather patterns or physical characteristics of an area.

Natural hazards such as flood, fire, earthquake, tornado, and windstorms affect thousands of people every year. We need to know what our risks are from natural hazards and take sensible precautions to protect ourselves, our families, and our communities.

Use the information contained in this chapter to learn about the hazards that pose a risk to you. Include the pertinent information in your family disaster plan. Specific content on each hazard consists of the characteristics of that hazard, terms associated with the hazard, measures that can be taken beforehand to avoid or lessen the impact of these events, and what individuals need to do during and after the event to protect themselves.

When you complete this chapter, you will be able to do the following:

- Know important terms.
- Take protective measures for natural hazards.

EARTHQUAKES

One of the most frightening and destructive phenomena of nature is a severe earthquake and its terrible aftereffects. An earthquake is a sudden movement of the earth, caused by the abrupt release of strain that has accumulated over a long time.

For hundreds of millions of years, the forces of plate tectonics have shaped the earth, as the huge plates that form the earth's surface slowly move over, under, and past each other. Sometimes, the movement is gradual. At other times, the plates are locked together, unable to release the accumulating energy. When the accumulated energy grows strong enough, the plates break free. If the earthquake occurs in a populated area, it may cause many deaths and injuries and extensive property damage.

Know the Terms

Familiarize yourself with these terms to help identify an earthquake hazard:

Earthquake—A sudden slipping or movement of a portion of the earth's crust, accompanied and followed by a series of vibrations.

Aftershock—An earthquake of similar or lesser intensity that follows the main earthquake.

Fault—The fracture across which displacement has occurred during an earthquake. The slippage may range from less than an inch to more than 10 yards, or about nine meters, in a severe earthquake.

Epicenter—The place on the earth's surface directly above the point on the fault where the earthquake rupture began. Once fault slippage begins, it expands along the fault during the earthquake and can extend hundreds of miles before stopping.

Seismic Waves—Vibrations that travel outward from the earthquake fault at speeds of several miles per second. Although fault slippage directly under a structure can cause considerable damage, the vibrations of seismic waves cause most of the destruction during earthquakes.

Magnitude—The amount of energy released during an earthquake, which is computed from the amplitude of the seismic waves. A magnitude of 7.0 on the Richter Scale indicates an extremely strong earthquake. Each whole number on the scale represents an increase of about 30 times more energy released than the previous whole number represents. Therefore, an earthquake measuring 6.0 is about 30 times more powerful than one measuring 5.0.

Take Protective Measures

Before an Earthquake

To protect yourself, your family, and your property in the event of an earthquake, do the following:

- Repair defective electrical wiring, leaky gas lines, and inflexible utility connections. Get appropriate professional help. Do not work with gas or electrical lines yourself.

- Bolt down and secure to the wall studs your water heater, refrigerator, furnace, and gas appliances. If recommended by your gas company, have an automatic gas shutoff valve installed that is triggered by strong vibrations.
- Place large or heavy objects on lower shelves. Fasten shelves, mirrors, and large picture frames to walls. Brace high and top-heavy objects.
- Store bottled foods, glass, china, and other breakables on low shelves or in cabinets that fasten shut.
- Anchor overhead lighting fixtures.
- Be sure the residence is firmly anchored to its foundation.
- Install flexible pipe fittings to avoid gas or water leaks. Flexible fittings are more resistant to breakage.
- Locate safe spots in each room under a sturdy table or against an inside wall. Reinforce this information by moving to these places during each drill.
- Hold earthquake drills with your family members: Drop, cover, and hold on!

During an Earthquake

Minimize your movements during an earthquake to a few steps to a nearby safe place. Stay indoors until the shaking has stopped and you are sure exiting is safe.

If You Are Indoors

- Take cover under a sturdy desk, table, or bench or against an inside wall, and hold on. If there isn't a table or desk near you, cover your face and head with your arms and crouch in an inside corner of the building.
- Stay away from glass, windows, outside doors and walls, and anything that could fall, such as lighting fixtures or furniture.
- If you are in bed when an earthquake strikes, stay there. Hold on and protect your head with a pillow, unless you are under a heavy light fixture that could fall. In that case, move to the nearest safe place.
- Use a doorway for shelter only if it is in close proximity to you and if you know it is a strongly supported, load bearing doorway.
- Stay inside until the shaking stops and it is safe to go outside. Most injuries during earthquakes occur when people are hit by falling objects when entering into or exiting from buildings.
- Be aware that the electricity may go out or the sprinkler systems or fire alarms may turn on.
- *Do not* use the elevators.

If You Are Outdoors

- Stay there.
- Move away from buildings, streetlights, and utility wires.

If You Are in a Moving Vehicle

- Stop as quickly as safety permits, and stay in the vehicle. Avoid stopping near or under buildings, trees, overpasses, and utility wires.
- Proceed cautiously once the earthquake has stopped, watching for road and bridge damage.

If You Are Trapped Under Debris

- *Do not* light a match.
- *Do not* move about unnecessarily or kick up dust.
- Cover your mouth with a handkerchief or clothing.
- Tap on a pipe or wall so rescuers can locate you. Use a whistle if one is available. Shout only as a last resort (shouting can cause you to inhale dangerous amounts of dust).

After an Earthquake

- Be prepared for aftershocks. These secondary shockwaves are usually less violent than the main quake but can be strong enough to do additional damage to weakened structures.
- Open cabinets cautiously. Beware of objects that can fall off shelves.
- Stay away from damaged areas unless your assistance has been specifically requested by police, fire, or relief organizations.
- Be aware of possible tsunamis if you live in coastal areas. These are also known as seismic sea waves (mistakenly called tidal waves). When local authorities issue a tsunami warning, assume that a series of dangerous waves is on the way. Stay away from the beach.

Review guidelines for Sheltering.

FIRES

Each year, more than 4,000 Americans die and more than 25,000 are injured in fires, many of which could be prevented. Direct property loss due to fires is estimated at $8.6 billion annually.

To protect yourself and your family, it is important to understand the basic characteristics of fire. Fire spreads quickly; there is no time to gather valuables or make a phone call. In just two minutes, a fire can become life-threatening. In five minutes, a residence can be engulfed in flames.

Heat and smoke from fire can be more dangerous than the flames. Inhaling the super-hot air can sear your lungs. Fire produces poisonous gases that make you disoriented and drowsy. Instead of being awakened by a fire, you may fall into a deeper sleep. Asphyxiation is the leading cause of fire deaths, exceeding burns by a three-to-one ratio.

Classification of Fires

Accepted standard practices separate fires into four general classes:

Class A—Fires of ordinary combustible materials where the so-called quenching and cooling effects of quantities of water or of solutions containing large quantities of water are of first importance. Examples are fires in wood, textile fabric, rubbish, or any material that leaves an ash.

Class B—Fires in combustible liquids, petroleum products, and so forth, where the blanketing or smothering effect of the extinguishing agent is of first importance. Examples are gas, oil, and grease fires. These substances may be stored in tanks, containers, or open vats, or they may be running freely on the ground.

Class C—Fires involving electrical equipment where the use of a nonconductive extinguishing agent is of first importance. Examples are fires involving electrical switchboards, motors, or wiring.

Class D—Fires involving flammable metals (for example, magnesium).

Generally, you should equip your vehicles with extinguisher(s) to provide the minimum rating required; 2A10-B:C means large enough to extinguish a fire of B:C class covering 10 square feet, or about one square meter, of surface.

Consider using type AB or type ABC fire extinguishers around your home or residence (at least one on each floor and at least one dry agent ABC fire extinguisher in the kitchen).

Take Protective Measures

Before a Fire

- Install smoke alarms. Properly working smoke alarms decrease your chances of dying in a fire by half.
- Place smoke alarms on every level of your residence. Place them outside bedrooms on the ceiling or high on the wall (4 to 12 inches, or about 20cm, from ceiling), at the top of open stairways, or at the bottom of enclosed stairs and near (but not in) the kitchen.
- Test and clean smoke alarms once a month and replace batteries at least once a year. Replace smoke alarms once every 10 years.

Escaping the Fire

- Review escape routes with your family. Practice escaping from each room.
- Make sure windows are not nailed or painted shut. Make sure security gratings on windows have a fire safety opening feature so they can be easily opened from the inside.
- Consider escape ladders if your residence has more than one level, and ensure that burglar bars and other antitheft mechanisms that block outside window entry are easily opened from the inside.

- Teach family members to stay low to the floor (where the air is safer in a fire) when escaping from a fire.
- Clean out storage areas. Do not let trash, such as old newspapers and magazines, accumulate.

Flammable Items

- Never use gasoline, benzene, naphtha, or similar flammable liquids indoors.
- Store flammable liquids in approved containers in well-ventilated storage areas.
- Never smoke near flammable liquids.
- Discard all rags or materials that have been soaked in flammable liquids after you have used them. Safely discard them outdoors in a metal container.
- Insulate chimneys and place spark arresters on top. The chimney should be at least three feet, or about one meter, higher than the roof. Remove branches hanging above and around the chimney.

Heating Sources

- Be careful when using alternative heating sources.
- Check with your local fire department on the legality of using kerosene heaters in your community. Be sure to fill kerosene heaters outside, and be sure they have cooled.
- Place heaters at least three feet, or about one meter, away from flammable materials. Make sure the floor and nearby walls are properly insulated.
- Use only the type of fuel designated for your unit and follow manufacturer's instructions.
- Store ashes in a metal container outside and away from your residence.
- Keep open flames away from walls, furniture, drapery, and flammable items.
- Keep a screen in front of the fireplace.
- Have heating units inspected and cleaned annually by a certified specialist.

Matches and Smoking

- Keep matches and lighters up high, away from children, and, if possible, in a locked cabinet.
- Never smoke in bed or when drowsy or medicated. Provide smokers with deep, sturdy ashtrays. Douse cigarette and cigar butts with water before disposal.

Electrical Wiring

- Have the electrical wiring in your residence checked by an electrician.
- Inspect extension cords for frayed or exposed wires or loose plugs.
- Make sure outlets have cover plates and no exposed wiring.
- Make sure wiring does not run under rugs, over nails, or across high-traffic areas.

- Do not overload extension cords or outlets. If you need to plug in two or three appliances, get a UL-approved unit with built-in circuit breakers to prevent sparks and short circuits.
- Make sure insulation does not touch bare electrical wiring.

Other

- Sleep with your door closed.
- Install ABC-type fire extinguishers in your residence, and teach family members how to use them.
- Consider installing an automatic fire sprinkler system in your residence.
- Ask your local fire department to inspect your residence for fire safety and prevention.

During a Fire

If your clothes catch on fire, you should do the following:

- Stop, drop, and roll—until the fire is extinguished. Running only makes the fire burn faster.

To escape a fire, you should:
- Check closed doors for heat before you open them. If you are escaping through a closed door, use the back of your hand to feel the top of the door, the doorknob, and the crack between the door and door frame before you open it. Never use the palm of your hand or fingers to test for heat (burning your hands could impair your ability to escape a fire using ladders and crawling).
  - **If the Door Is Hot**—*Do not* open it. Escape through a window. If you cannot escape, hang a white or light-colored sheet outside the window, alerting firefighters to your presence.
  - **If the Door Is Cool**—Open slowly and ensure fire and/or smoke is not blocking your escape route. If your escape route is blocked, shut the door immediately and use an alternate escape route, such as a window. If clear, leave immediately through the door, and close it behind you. Be prepared to crawl. Smoke and heat rise. The air is clearer and cooler near the floor.
- Crawl low under any smoke to your exit—heavy smoke and poisonous gases collect first along the ceiling.
- Close doors behind you as you escape to delay the spread of the fire.
- Stay out once you are safely out. *Do not* reenter. Call 9-1-1.

After a Fire

Listed below are guidelines for different circumstances in the period following a fire:

- If you are with burn victims, or are a burn victim yourself, call 9-1-1; cool and cover burns to reduce chance of further injury or infection.

- If you detect heat or smoke when entering a damaged building, evacuate immediately.
- If you are a tenant, contact the landlord.
- If you have a safe or strong box, do not try to open it. It can hold intense heat for several hours. If the door is opened before the box has cooled, the contents could burst into flames.
- If you must leave your home because a building inspector says the building is unsafe, ask someone you trust to watch the property during your absence.
- Follow the instructions for recovering from a disaster in Chapter 7.

FLOODS

Floods are one of the most common hazards in the United States. Flood effects can be local, impacting a neighborhood or community, or very large, affecting entire river basins and multiple states.

However, all floods are not alike. Some floods develop slowly, sometimes over a period of days. But flash floods can develop quickly, sometimes in just a few minutes and without any visible signs of rain. Flash floods often have a dangerous wall of roaring water that carries rocks, mud, and other debris and can sweep away most things in its path. Overland flooding occurs outside a defined river or stream, such as when a levee is breached, but still can be destructive. Flooding can also occur when a dam breaks, producing effects similar to flash floods.

Be aware of flood hazards no matter where you live, but especially if you live in a low-lying area, near water or downstream from a dam. Even very small streams, gullies, creeks, culverts, dry streambeds, or low-lying ground that appears harmless in dry weather can flood. Every state is at risk from this hazard.

Know the Terms

Familiarize yourself with these terms to help identify a flood hazard:

Flood Watch—Flooding is possible; tune in to NOAA Weather Radio, commercial radio, or television for information.

Flash Flood Watch—Flash flooding is possible; be prepared to move to higher ground; listen to NOAA Weather Radio, commercial radio, or television for information.

Flood Warning—Flooding is occurring or will occur soon; if advised to evacuate, do so immediately.

Flash Flood Warning—A flash flood is occurring; seek higher ground on foot immediately.

Take Protective Measures

Before a Flood

To prepare for a flood, you should consider the following:

- Avoid building in a floodplain unless you elevate and reinforce your home.
- Elevate the furnace, water heater, and electric panel if susceptible to flooding.
- Install check valves in sewer traps to prevent flood water from backing up into the drains of your home.
- Construct barriers (levees, beams, floodwalls) to stop floodwater from entering the building.
- Seal walls in basements with waterproofing compounds to avoid seepage.

During a Flood

If a flood is likely in your area, you should do the following:

- Listen to the radio or television for information.
- Be aware that flash flooding can occur. If there is any possibility of a flash flood, move immediately to higher ground. Do not wait for instructions to move.
- Be aware of streams, drainage channels, canyons, and other areas known to flood suddenly. Flash floods can occur in these areas with or without such typical warnings as rain clouds or heavy rain.

If you must prepare to evacuate, you should take these steps:

- Secure your home. If you have time, bring in outdoor furniture. Move essential items to an upper floor.
- Turn off utilities at the main switches or valves if instructed to do so. Disconnect electrical appliances. *Do not* touch electrical equipment if you are wet or standing in water.

If you have to leave your home, remember these evacuation tips:

- Do not walk through moving water. Six inches, or about 15 cm, of moving water can make you fall. If you have to walk in water, walk where the water is not moving. Use a stick to check the firmness of the ground in front of you.
- Do not drive into flooded areas. If floodwaters rise around your car, abandon the car and move to higher ground if you can do so safely. You and the vehicle can be quickly swept away.

After a Flood

Guidelines for the period following a flood are as follows:

- Listen for news reports to learn whether the community's water supply is safe to drink.

- Avoid floodwaters; water may be contaminated by oil, gasoline, or raw sewage. Water may also be electrically charged from underground or downed power lines.
- Avoid moving water.
- Be aware of areas where floodwaters have receded. Roads may have weakened and could collapse under the weight of a car.
- Stay away from downed power lines, and report them to the power company.
- Return home only when authorities indicate it is safe.
- Stay out of any building if it is surrounded by floodwaters.
- Use extreme caution when entering buildings; there may be hidden damage, particularly in foundations.
- Service damaged septic tanks, cesspools, pits, and leaching systems as soon as possible. Damaged sewage systems are serious health hazards.
- Clean and disinfect everything that got wet. Mud left from floodwater can contain sewage and chemicals.

Review guidelines for Sheltering.

Driving: Flood Facts

Important points to remember when driving in flood conditions:

- Six inches, or about 15cm, of water will reach the bottom of most passenger cars causing loss of control and possible stalling.
- A foot, or about 30cm, of water will float many vehicles.
- Two feet, or about 60cm, of rushing water can carry away most vehicles including sport utility vehicles (SUV's) and pickups.

EXTREME HEAT

Heat kills by pushing the human body beyond its limits. In extreme heat and high humidity, evaporation is slowed, and the body must work extra hard to maintain a normal temperature.

Most heat disorders occur because the victim has been overexposed to heat or has overexercised for his or her age and physical condition. Older adults, young children, and those who are sick or overweight are more likely to succumb to extreme heat.

Conditions that can induce heat-related illnesses include stagnant atmospheric conditions and poor air quality. Consequently, people living in urban areas may be at greater risk from the effects of a prolonged heat wave than those living in rural areas. Also, asphalt and concrete store heat longer and gradually release heat at night, which can produce higher nighttime temperatures known as the urban heat island effect.

Know the Terms

Familiarize yourself with these terms to help identify an extreme heat hazard:

Heat Wave—Prolonged period of excessive heat, often combined with excessive humidity.

Heat Index—A number in degrees Fahrenheit (F) that tells how hot it feels when relative humidity is added to the air temperature. Exposure to full sunshine can increase the heat index by 15 degrees.

Heat Cramps—Muscular pains and spasms due to heavy exertion. Although heat cramps are the least severe, they are often the first signal that the body is having trouble with the heat.

Heat Exhaustion—Typically occurs when people exercise heavily or work in a hot, humid place where body fluids are lost through heavy sweating. Blood flow to the skin increases, causing blood flow to decrease to the vital organs. This results in a form of mild shock. If not treated, the victim's condition will worsen. Body temperature will keep rising and the victim may suffer heatstroke.

Heatstroke—A life-threatening condition; the victim's temperature control system, which produces sweating to cool the body, stops working. The body temperature can rise so high that brain damage and death may result if the body is not cooled quickly.

Sunstroke—Another term for heatstroke.

Take Protective Measures

Before Extreme Heat

To prepare for extreme heat, you should take the following precautions:

- Install window air conditioners snugly; insulate if necessary.
- Check air-conditioning ducts for proper insulation.
- Install temporary window reflectors (for use between windows and drapes), such as aluminum-foil-covered cardboard, to reflect heat back outside.
- Weather-strip doors and sills to keep cool air in.
- Cover windows that receive morning or afternoon sun with drapes, shades, awnings, or louvers. (Outdoor awnings or louvers can reduce the heat that enters a home by up to 80 percent.)
- Keep storm windows up all year.

During a Heat Emergency

Guidelines for what you should do if the weather is extremely hot are as follows:

- Stay indoors as much as possible, and limit exposure to the sun.

- Stay on the lowest floor out of the sunshine if air conditioning is not available.
- Consider spending the warmest part of the day in public buildings such as libraries, schools, movie theaters, shopping malls, and other community facilities. Circulating air can cool the body by increasing the perspiration rate of evaporation.
- Eat well-balanced, light, and regular meals. Avoid using salt tablets unless directed to do so by a physician.
- Drink plenty of water. Persons who have epilepsy or heart, kidney, or liver disease; are on fluid-restricted diets; or have a problem with fluid retention should consult a doctor before increasing liquid intake.
- Limit intake of alcoholic beverages.
- Dress in loose-fitting, lightweight, and light-colored clothes that cover as much skin as possible.
- Protect face and head by wearing a wide-brimmed hat.
- Check on family, friends, and neighbors who do not have air conditioning and who spend much of their time alone.
- Never leave children or pets alone in closed vehicles.
- Avoid strenuous work during the warmest part of the day. Use a buddy system when working in extreme heat, and take frequent breaks.

First Aid for Heat-Induced Illnesses

Extreme heat brings with it the possibility of heat-induced illnesses.

Additional Information

An emergency water shortage can be caused by prolonged drought, poor water supply management, or contamination of a surface water supply source or aquifer. Drought can affect vast territorial regions and large population numbers. Drought also creates environmental conditions that increase the risk of other hazards such as fire, flash flood, and possible landslides and mudslides.

Conserving water means more water available for critical needs for everyone. The Appendix contains detailed suggestions for conserving water both indoors and outdoors. Make these practices a part of your daily life and help preserve this essential resource.

After Extreme Heat

Follow the instructions for recovering from a disaster in Chapter 7.

HURRICANES

A hurricane is a type of *tropical cyclone*, the generic term for a low pressure system that generally forms in the tropics. A typical cyclone is accompanied

Table 4.1
First Aid for Heat-Induced Illness

Condition	Symptoms	First aid
Sunburn	Skin redness and pain, possible swelling, blisters, fever, headaches	• The victim should take a shower using soap to remove oils that may block pores, preventing the body from cooling naturally. • Apply dry, sterile dressings to any blisters, and get medical attention.
Heat cramps	Painful spasms, usually in leg and abdominal muscles; heavy sweating	• Get the victim to a cooler location. • Lightly stretch and gently massage affected muscles to relieve spasms. • Give sips of up to a half glass of cool water every 15 minutes. (Do not give liquids with caffeine or alcohol.) • Discontinue liquids if victim is nauseated.
Heat exhaustion	Heavy sweating, but skin may be cool, pale, or flushed; weak pulse; normal body temperature is possible, but temperature will likely rise; possible fainting or dizziness, nausea, vomiting, exhaustion, and headaches	• Lie victim down in a cool place. • Loosen or remove clothing. • Apply cool, wet cloths. • Give sips of water if victim is conscious. • Be sure victim consumes water slowly. • Give a half glass of cool water every 15 minutes. • Discontinue water if victim is nauseated.
Heat stroke	High body temperature (105+ degrees Fahrenheit or 40+ degrees Celsius); hot, red, dry skin; rapid, weak pulse; rapid, shallow breathing; victim will probably not sweat unless sweating from recent strenuous activity; possible unconsciousness	• Call 9-1-1 or emergency medical services, or get the victim to a hospital immediately. Delay can be fatal. • Lie victim down in a cool place. • Remove clothing. • Try a cool bath, sponging, or wet sheet to reduce body temperature. • Watch for breathing problems. • Use extreme caution. • Use fans and air conditioners.

by thunderstorms, and in the Northern Hemisphere, a counterclockwise circulation of winds near the earth's surface.

All Atlantic and Gulf of Mexico coastal areas are subject to hurricanes or tropical storms. Parts of the Southwest United States and the Pacific Coast experience heavy rains and floods each year from hurricanes spawned off Mexico. The Atlantic hurricane season lasts from June to November, with the peak season from mid-August to late October.

Hurricanes can cause catastrophic damage to coastlines and several hundred miles inland. Winds can exceed 155 miles per hour. Hurricanes and tropical storms can also spawn tornadoes and microbursts, create storm surges along the coast, and cause extensive damage from heavy rainfall.

Hurricanes are classified into five categories based on their wind speed, central pressure, and damage potential (see chart). Category Three and higher hurricanes are considered major hurricanes, though Categories One and Two are still extremely dangerous and warrant your full attention.

Hurricanes can produce widespread torrential rains. Floods are the deadly and destructive result. Slow moving storms and tropical storms moving into mountainous regions tend to produce especially heavy rain. Excessive rain can trigger landslides or mudslides, especially in mountainous regions. Flash flooding can occur due to intense rainfall. Flooding on rivers and streams may persist for several days or more after the storm.

Between 1970 and 1999, more people lost their lives from freshwater inland flooding associated with land falling tropical cyclones than from any

Table 4.2
Saffir-Simpson Hurricane Scale

Class	Sustained winds	Damage	Storm surge
1	74–95 mph	**Minimal**—Unanchored mobile homes, vegetation, and signs	4–5 feet
2	96–110 mph	**Moderate**—All mobile homes, roofs, small craft; flooding	6–8 feet
3	111–130 mph	**Extensive**—Small buildings; low-lying roads cut off	9–12 feet
4	131–155 mph	**Extreme**—Roofs destroyed, trees down, roads cut off, mobile homes destroyed, beach homes flooded	13–18 feet
5	>155 mph	**Catastrophic**—Most buildings destroyed, vegetation destroyed, major roads cut off, homes flooded	>18 feet

other weather hazard related to tropical cyclones. Do not underestimate the potential for flooding and the resulting hazards.

Know the Terms

Familiarize yourself with these terms to help identify a hurricane hazard:

Tropical Depression—An organized system of clouds and thunderstorms with a defined surface circulation and maximum sustained winds of 38 mph (33 knots), or about 61 kph, or less. Sustained winds are defined as one-minute average wind measured at about 33 feet (10 meters) above the surface.

Tropical Storm—An organized system of strong thunderstorms with a defined surface circulation and maximum sustained winds of 39–73 mph (34–63 knots), or up to about 118 kph.

Hurricane—An intense tropical weather system of strong thunderstorms with a well defined surface circulation and maximum sustained winds of 74 MPH (64 knots) or higher.

Storm Surge—A dome of water pushed onshore by hurricane and tropical storm winds. Storm surges can reach 25 feet high, or about 7.6 meters, and be 50–100 miles, or up to about 160 km, wide.

Storm Tide—A combination of storm surge and the normal tide (for example, a 15-foot, or 4.5-meter, storm surge combined with a 2-foot, or 0.6-meter, normal high tide over the mean sea level creates a 17-foot, or about 5.2-meter, storm tide).

Hurricane/Tropical Storm Watch—Hurricane/tropical storm conditions are possible in the specified area, usually within 36 hours. Tune in to NOAA Weather Radio, commercial radio, or television for information.

Hurricane/Tropical Storm Warning—Hurricane/tropical storm conditions are expected in the specified area, usually within 24 hours.

Short-Term Watches and Warnings—These warnings provide detailed information about specific hurricane threats, such as flash floods and tornadoes.

Take Protective Measures

Before a Hurricane

To prepare for a hurricane, take the following steps:

- Make plans to secure your property. Permanent storm shutters offer the best protection for windows. A second option is to board up windows with 5/8 inch, or 16mm, thick marine plywood, cut to fit and ready to install. Tape does not prevent windows from breaking.
- Install straps or additional clips to securely fasten your roof to the frame structure. This will reduce roof damage.
- Be sure trees and shrubs around your home are well trimmed.
- Clear loose and clogged rain gutters and downspouts.

- Determine how and where to secure your boat.
- Consider building a safe room.

During a Hurricane

If a hurricane is likely in your area, you should do the following:

- Listen to the radio or TV for information.
- Secure your home, close storm shutters, and secure outdoor objects or bring them indoors.
- Turn off utilities if instructed to do so. Otherwise, turn the refrigerator thermostat to its coldest setting and keep its doors closed.
- Turn off propane tanks.
- Avoid using the phone, except for serious emergencies.
- Moor your boat if time permits.
- Ensure a supply of water for sanitary purposes such as cleaning and flushing toilets. Fill the bathtub and other large containers with water.

You should evacuate:

- If you are directed by local authorities to do so. Be sure to follow their instructions.
- If you live in a mobile home or temporary structure—such shelters are particularly hazardous during hurricanes no matter how well fastened to the ground.
- If you live in a high-rise building—hurricane winds are stronger at higher elevations.
- If you live on the coast, on a floodplain, near a river, or on an inland waterway.
- If you feel you are in danger.

If you are unable to evacuate, go to your wind-safe room. If you do not have one, follow these guidelines:

- Stay indoors during the hurricane and away from windows and glass doors.
- Close all interior doors—secure and brace external doors.
- Keep curtains and blinds closed. Do not be fooled if there is a lull; it could be the eye of the storm—winds will pick up again.
- Take refuge in a small interior room, closet, or hallway on the lowest level.
- Lie on the floor under a table or another sturdy object.

After a Hurricane

Follow the instructions for recovering from a disaster in Chapter 7. Review guidelines for Sheltering.

LANDSLIDES AND MUDSLIDES

Landslides occur in all U.S. states and territories. In a landslide, masses of rock, earth, or debris move down a slope. Landslides may be small or large, slow or rapid. They are activated by storms, earthquakes, volcanic eruptions, fires, and human modification of land.

Debris and mudflows are rivers of rock, earth, and other debris saturated with water. They develop when water rapidly accumulates in the ground, during heavy rainfall or rapid snowmelt, changing the earth into a flowing river of mud or slurry. They flow can rapidly, striking with little or no warning at avalanche speeds. They also can travel several miles from their source, growing in size as they pick up trees, boulders, cars, and other materials.

Landslide problems can be caused by land mismanagement, particularly in mountain, canyon, and coastal regions. Land-use zoning, professional inspections, and proper design can minimize many landslide, mudflow, and debris flow problems.

Take Protective Measures

Before a Landslide or Mudslide

Steps you can take to protect yourself from the effects of a landslide or mudflow are listed below:

- Do not build near steep slopes, close to mountain edges, near drainage ways, or natural erosion valleys.
- Get a ground assessment of your property.
- Consult an appropriate professional expert for advice on corrective measures.
- Minimize home hazards by having flexible pipe fittings installed to avoid gas or water leaks, as flexible fittings are more resistant to breakage (only the gas company or professionals should install gas fittings).

Recognize Landslide Warning Signs

- Changes occur in your landscape such as patterns of storm-water drainage on slopes (especially the places where runoff water converges) land movement, small slides, flows, or progressively leaning trees.
- Doors or windows stick or jam for the first time.
- New cracks appear in plaster, tile, brick, or foundations.
- Outside walls, walks, or stairs begin pulling away from the building.
- Slowly developing, widening cracks appear on the ground or on paved areas such as streets or driveways.
- Underground utility lines break.
- Bulging ground appears at the base of a slope.
- Water breaks through the ground surface in new locations.

- Fences, retaining walls, utility poles, or trees tilt or move.
- A faint rumbling sound that increases in volume is noticeable as the landslide nears.
- The ground slopes downward in one direction and may begin shifting in that direction under your feet.
- Unusual sounds, such as trees cracking or boulders knocking together, might indicate moving debris.
- Collapsed pavement, mud, fallen rocks, and other indications of possible debris flow can be seen when driving (embankments along roadsides are particularly susceptible to landslides).

During a Landslide or Mudslide

Guidelines for what you should do if a landslide or mudflow occurs:

- Move away from the path of a landslide or mudflow as quickly as possible.
- Curl into a tight ball, and protect your head if escape is not possible.

After a Landslide or Mudslide

Guidelines for what you should do during the period following a landslide:

- Stay away from the slide area. There may be danger of additional slides.
- Check for injured and trapped persons near the slide, without entering the direct slide area; direct rescuers to their locations.
- Watch for associated dangers such as broken electrical, water, gas, and sewage lines and damaged roadways and railways.
- Replant damaged ground as soon as possible since erosion caused by loss of ground cover can lead to flash flooding and additional landslides in the near future.
- Seek advice from a geotechnical expert for evaluating landslide hazards or designing corrective techniques to reduce landslide risk.
- Follow the instructions for recovering from a disaster in Chapter 7.

THUNDERSTORMS AND LIGHTNING

All thunderstorms are dangerous. Every thunderstorm produces lightning. Each year in the United States, about 300 people are injured and 80 people are killed by lightning. Although most lightning victims survive, people struck by lightning often report a variety of long-term, debilitating symptoms.

Other associated dangers of thunderstorms include tornadoes, strong winds, hail, and flash flooding. Flash flooding is responsible for more fatalities—more than 140 annually—than any other thunderstorm-associated hazard.

Dry thunderstorms that do not produce rain that reaches the ground are most prevalent in the western United States. Falling raindrops evaporate, but lightning can still reach the ground and can start wildfires.

Facts about thunderstorms:

- They may occur singly, in clusters, or in lines.
- Some of the most severe occur when a single thunderstorm affects one location for an extended time.
- Thunderstorms typically produce heavy rain for a brief period, anywhere from 30 minutes to an hour.
- Warm, humid conditions are highly favorable for thunderstorm development.
- About 10 percent of thunderstorms are classified as severe—one that produces hail at least three-quarters of an inch, or about 19mm, in diameter, has winds of 58 mph, or about 93 kph, or higher, or produces a tornado.

Facts about lightning:

- Lightning's unpredictability increases the risk to individuals and property.
- Lightning often strikes outside of heavy rain and may occur as far as 10 miles away from any rainfall.
- So-called heat lightning is actually lightning from a thunderstorm too far away for thunder to be heard. However, the storm may be moving in your direction!
- Most lightning deaths and injuries occur when people are caught outdoors in the summer months during the afternoon and evening.
- Your chances of being struck by lightning are estimated to be 1 in 600,000, but could be reduced even further by following safety precautions.
- Lightning strike victims carry no electrical charge and should be attended to immediately.

Know the Terms

Familiarize yourself with these terms to help identify a thunderstorm hazard:

Severe Thunderstorm Watch—Tells you when and where severe thunderstorms are likely to occur. Watch the sky and stay tuned to NOAA Weather Radio, commercial radio, or television for information.

Severe Thunderstorm Warning—Issued when severe weather has been reported by spotters or indicated by radar. Warnings indicate imminent danger to life and property to those in the path of the storm.

Take Protective Measures

Before Thunderstorms and Lightning

To prepare for a thunderstorm, you should take the following precautions:

- Remove dead or rotting trees and branches that could fall and cause injury or damage during a severe thunderstorm.

- Remember the 30/30 lightning safety rule: Go indoors if, after seeing lightning, you cannot count to 30 before hearing thunder. Stay indoors for 30 minutes after hearing the last clap of thunder.

Thunderstorms

If a thunderstorm is likely in your area, follow these guidelines:

- Postpone outdoor activities.
- Get inside a home, building, or hard top automobile (not a convertible). Although you may be injured if lightning strikes your car, you are much safer inside a vehicle than outside.
- Remember, rubber-soled shoes and rubber tires provide *no* protection from lightning. However, the steel frame of a hard-topped vehicle provides increased protection if you are not touching metal.
- Secure outdoor objects that could blow away or cause damage.
- Shutter windows and secure outside doors. If shutters are not available, close window blinds, shades, or curtains.
- Avoid showering or bathing. Plumbing and bathroom fixtures can conduct electricity.
- Use a corded telephone only for emergencies. Cordless and cellular telephones are safe to use.
- Unplug appliances and other electrical items such as computers and turn off air conditioners. Power surges from lightning can cause serious damage.
- Use your battery-operated NOAA Weather Radio for updates from local officials.

You should avoid the following:

- Natural lightning rods such as a tall, isolated tree in an open area.
- Hilltops, open fields, the beach, or a boat on the water.
- Isolated sheds or other small structures in open areas.
- Anything metal—tractors, farm equipment, motorcycles, golf carts, golf clubs, and bicycles.

During a Thunderstorm

- **If You Are Outside Under Trees**—Seek shelter in a low area under a thick growth of small trees.
- **If You Are Outside in an Open Area**—Go to a low place such as a ravine or valley. Be alert for flash floods.
- **If You Are on Open Water**—Get to land and find shelter fast.
- **If You Feel Your Hair Stand on End**—This is an indication that the air around you is ionized and lightning is about to strike. Squat low to the ground on the balls of your feet. Place your hands over your ears and your head between your knees. Make yourself the smallest target possible and minimize your contact with the ground. *Do not* lie flat on the ground.

After a Thunderstorm

If somebody is injured, call 9-1-1 for medical assistance as soon as possible. When you attempt to give aid to a victim of lightning, you should check the following:

- **Breathing**—If breathing has stopped, begin mouth-to-mouth resuscitation.
- **Heartbeat**—If the heart has stopped, administer CPR.
- **Pulse**—If the victim has a pulse and is breathing, look for other possible injuries. Check for burns where the lightning entered and left the body. Also be alert for nervous system damage, broken bones, and loss of hearing and eyesight.

TORNADOES

Tornadoes are nature's most violent storms. Spawned from powerful thunderstorms, tornadoes can cause fatalities and devastate a neighborhood in seconds. A tornado appears as a rotating, funnel-shaped cloud that extends from a thunderstorm to the ground with whirling winds that can reach 300 miles per hour or 483 kilometers per hour. Damage paths can be in excess of 1 mile wide (about 1.6 km) and 50 miles long (about 80 km). Every state is at some risk from this hazard.

Some tornadoes are clearly visible, while rain or nearby low-hanging clouds obscure others. Occasionally, tornadoes develop so rapidly that little, if any, advance warning is possible.

Before a tornado hits, the wind may die down and the air may become very still. A cloud of debris can mark the location of a tornado even if a funnel is not visible. Tornadoes generally occur near the trailing edge of a thunderstorm. It is not uncommon to see clear, sunlit skies behind a tornado.

Facts about tornadoes:

- They may strike quickly, with little or no warning.
- They may appear nearly transparent until dust and debris are picked up or a cloud forms in the funnel.
- The average tornado moves southwest to northeast, but tornadoes can move in any direction.
- The average forward speed of a tornado is 30 mph, or about 48 kph, but may vary from stationary to 70 mph, or about 113 kph.
- Tornadoes can accompany tropical storms and hurricanes as they move onto land.
- Waterspouts are tornadoes that form over water.
- Tornadoes are most frequently reported east of the Rocky Mountains during spring and summer months.
- Peak tornado season in the southern states is March through May; in the northern states, it is late spring through early summer.
- Tornadoes are most likely to occur between 3 P.M. and 9 P.M., but can occur at any time.

Know the Terms

Familiarize yourself with these terms to help identify a tornado hazard:

Tornado Watch—Tornadoes are possible. Remain alert for approaching storms. Watch the sky and stay tuned to NOAA Weather Radio, commercial radio, or television for information.

Tornado Warning—A tornado has been sighted or indicated by weather radar. Take shelter immediately.

Take Protective Measures

Before a Tornado

Be alert to changing weather conditions as follows:

- Listen to NOAA Weather Radio or to commercial radio or television newscasts for the latest information.
- Look for approaching storms.
- Look for the following danger signs:
  - Dark, often greenish sky
  - Large hail
  - A large, dark, low-lying cloud (particularly if rotating)
  - Loud roar, similar to a freight train

If you see approaching storms or any of the danger signs, be prepared to take shelter immediately.

During a Tornado

If you hear a tornado *warning*, seek shelter immediately!

- **If You Are Inside a Building**—Go to a predesignated shelter area such as a safe room, basement, storm cellar, or the lowest building level.
  - If there is no basement, go to the center of an interior room on the lowest level (closet, interior hallway) away from corners, windows, doors, and outside walls. Put as many walls as possible between you and the outside. Get under a sturdy table and use your arms to protect your head and neck.
  - *Do not* open windows.
- **If You Are in a Vehicle or Mobile Home**—Get out immediately and go to the lowest floor of a sturdy, nearby building or a storm shelter. Mobile homes, even if tied down, offer little protection from tornadoes.
- **If You Are Outside**—Lie flat in a nearby ditch or depression and cover your head with your hands. Be aware of the potential for flooding.
  - *Do not* get under an overpass or bridge. You are safer in a low, flat location.
  - Never try to outrun a tornado in urban or congested areas in a car or truck. Instead, leave the vehicle immediately for safe shelter.

- Watch out for flying debris. Flying debris from tornadoes causes most fatalities and injuries.

Preparing a Safe Room

Extreme windstorms in many parts of the country pose a serious threat to buildings and their occupants. Your residence may be built to code, but that does not mean it can withstand winds from extreme events such as tornadoes and major hurricanes. The purpose of a safe room or a wind shelter is to provide a space where you and your family can seek refuge that provides a high level of protection.

You can build a safe room in one of several places in your home:

- Your basement
- Atop a concrete slab-on-grade foundation or garage floor
- An interior room on the first floor

Safe rooms built below ground level provide the greatest protection, but a safe room built in a first-floor interior room also can provide the necessary protection. Below-ground safe rooms must be designed to avoid accumulating water during the heavy rains that often accompany severe windstorms.

To protect its occupants, a safe room must be built to withstand high winds and flying debris, even if the rest of the residence is severely damaged or destroyed.

Considerations for building a safe room include the following:

- The safe room must be adequately anchored to resist overturning and uplift.
- The walls, ceiling, and door of the shelter must withstand wind pressure and resist penetration by windborne objects and falling debris.
- The connections between all parts of the safe room must be strong enough to resist the wind.
- Sections of either interior or exterior residence walls that are used as walls of the safe room must be separated from the structure of the residence so that damage to the residence will not cause damage to the safe room.

TSUNAMIS

Tsunamis (pronounced soo-ná-mees), also known as seismic sea waves (mistakenly called tidal waves), are a series of enormous waves created by an underwater disturbance such as an earthquake, landslide, volcanic eruption, or meteorite. A tsunami can move hundreds of miles per hour in the open ocean and smash into land with waves as high as 100 feet, or 30 meters, or more.

From the area where the tsunami originates, waves travel outward in all directions. Once the wave approaches the shore, it builds in height. The topography of the coastline and the ocean floor will influence the size of the wave. There may be more than one wave and the succeeding one may be larger than the one before. That is why a small tsunami at one beach can be a giant wave a few miles away.

All tsunamis are potentially dangerous, even though they may not damage every coastline they strike. A tsunami can strike anywhere along most of the U.S. coastline. The most destructive tsunamis have occurred along the coasts of California, Oregon, Washington, Alaska, and Hawaii.

Earthquake-induced movement of the ocean floor most often generates tsunamis. If a major earthquake or landslide occurs close to shore, the first wave in a series could reach the beach in a few minutes, even before a warning is issued. Areas are at greater risk if they are less than 25 feet, or 7.6 meters, above sea level and within a mile, or about 1.6 km, of the shoreline. Drowning is the most common cause of death associated with a tsunami. Tsunami waves and the receding water are very destructive to structures in the run-up zone. Other hazards include flooding, contamination of drinking water, and fires from gas lines or ruptured tanks.

Know the Terms

Familiarize yourself with these terms to help identify a tsunami hazard:

Advisory—An earthquake has occurred in the Pacific basin, which might generate a tsunami.

Watch—A tsunami was or may have been generated, but is at least two hours travel time to the area in Watch status.

Warning—A tsunami was, or may have been generated, which could cause damage; therefore, people in the warned area are strongly advised to evacuate.

Take Protective Measures

During a Tsunami

If a tsunami is likely to occur in your area, take these precautions:

- Turn on your radio to learn if there is a tsunami warning if an earthquake occurs and you are in a coastal area.
- Move inland to higher ground immediately and stay there.
- If there is noticeable recession in water away from the shoreline this is nature's tsunami warning, and it should be heeded. You should move away immediately.

After a Tsunami

During the period following a tsunami, follow these guidelines:

- Stay away from flooded and damaged areas until officials say it is safe to return.
- Stay away from debris in the water; it may pose a safety hazard to boats and people.

Save Yourself—Not Your Possessions

No possession is worth your life. It is important to get to higher ground away from the coast and stay there until it is safe to return. Your neighbors will likely retreat to higher ground too, so you should be prepared for crowding conditions and overburdened resources. Review guidelines for Sheltering.

VOLCANOES

A volcano is a vent through which molten rock escapes to the earth's surface. When pressure from gases within the molten rock becomes too great, an eruption occurs. Eruptions can be quiet or explosive. There may be lava flows, flattened landscapes, poisonous gases, and flying rock and ash.

Because of their intense heat, lava flows are great fire hazards. Lava flows destroy everything in their path, but most move slowly enough that people can move out of the way.

Fresh volcanic ash, made of pulverized rock, can be abrasive, acidic, gritty, gassy, and odorous. While not immediately dangerous to most adults, the acidic gas and ash can cause lung damage to small infants, to older adults, and to those suffering from severe respiratory illnesses. Volcanic ash also can damage machinery, including engines and electrical equipment. Ash accumulations mixed with water become heavy and can collapse roofs.

Volcanic eruptions can be accompanied by other natural hazards, including earthquakes, mudflows and flash floods, rock falls and landslides, acid rain, fire, and (under special conditions) tsunamis. Active volcanoes in the United States are found mainly in Hawaii, Alaska, and the Pacific Northwest.

Take Protective Measures

Before a Volcanic Eruption

- Add a pair of goggles and a disposable breathing mask for each member of the family to your disaster supplies kit.
- Stay away from active volcano sites.

During a Volcanic Eruption

If a volcano erupts in your area, follow these guidelines:

- Evacuate immediately from the volcano area to avoid flying debris, hot gases, lateral blast, and lava flow.
- Be aware of mudflows. The danger from a mudflow increases near stream channels and with prolonged heavy rains. Mudflows can move faster than you can walk or run. Look upstream before crossing a bridge, and do not cross the bridge if mudflow is approaching.
- Avoid river valleys and low-lying areas.

Protection from Falling Ash

- Wear long-sleeved shirts and long pants.
- Use goggles and wear eyeglasses instead of contact lenses.
- Use a dust mask or hold a damp cloth over your face to help with breathing.
- Stay away from areas downwind from the volcano to avoid volcanic ash.
- Stay indoors until the ash has settled unless there is danger of the roof collapsing.
- Close doors, windows, and all ventilation in the house (chimney vents, furnaces, air conditioners, fans, and other vents).
- Clear heavy ash from fl at or low-pitched roofs and rain gutters.
- Avoid running car or truck engines. Driving can stir up volcanic ash that can clog engines, damage moving parts, and stall vehicles.
- Avoid driving in heavy ash fall unless absolutely required. If you have to drive, keep speed down to 35 mph, or about 56 kph, or slower.

After a Volcanic Eruption

Do not return to your home until authorities declare conditions safe. Follow the instructions for recovering from a disaster in Chapter 7.

WILDFIRES

If you live on a remote hillside or in a valley, prairie, or forest where flammable vegetation is abundant, your residence could be vulnerable to wildfires. These fires are usually triggered by lightning or accidents. Wildfires spread quickly, igniting brush, trees, and homes.

Take Protective Measures

Before a Wildfire

To prepare for wildfires, you should take the following precautions:

- Mark the entrance to your property with address signs that are clearly visible from the road.
- Keep lawns trimmed, leaves raked, and the roof and rain gutters free from debris such as dead limbs and leaves.
- Stack firewood at least 30 feet, or over nine meters, away from your residence.
- Store flammable materials, liquids, and solvents in metal containers outside your residence at least 30 feet, or over nine meters, away from structures and wooden fences.
- Create defensible space by thinning trees and brush within 30 feet or about nine meters around your residence. Beyond 30 feet, or about nine meters, remove dead wood, debris, and low tree branches.

- Landscape your property with fire resistant plants and vegetation to prevent fire from spreading quickly. For example, hardwood trees are more fire-resistant than pine, evergreen, eucalyptus, or fir trees.
- Make sure water sources, such as hydrants, ponds, swimming pools, and wells, are accessible to the fire department.
- Use fire resistant, protective roofing and materials like stone, brick, and metal to protect your residence. Avoid using wood materials. They offer the least fire protection.
- Cover all exterior vents, attics, and eaves with metal mesh screens no larger than 6 millimeters or 1/4 inch to prevent debris from collecting and to help keep sparks out.
- Install multipane windows, tempered safety glass, or fireproof shutters to protect large windows from radiant heat.
- Use fire-resistant draperies for added window protection.
- Have chimneys, wood stoves, and all home heating systems inspected and cleaned annually by a certified specialist.
- Insulate chimneys and place spark arresters on top. The chimney should be at least 3 feet, or about one meter, above the roof.
- Remove branches hanging above and around the chimney.

Follow Local Burning Laws

Before burning debris in a wooded area, make sure you notify local authorities, obtain a burning permit, and follow these guidelines:

- Use an approved incinerator with a safety lid or covering with holes no larger than 3/4 inch, or about 19mm.
- Create at least a 10-foot, or over three meter, clearing around the incinerator before burning debris.
- Have a fire extinguisher or garden hose on hand when burning debris.

During a Wildfire

If a wildfire threatens your home and time permits, do the following:

- Shut off gas at the meter. Only a qualified professional can safely turn the gas back on.
- Seal attic and ground vents with precut plywood or commercial seals.
- Turn off propane tanks (remove them from the vicinity of your home).
- Place combustible patio furniture inside.
- Connect garden hose to outside taps. Place lawn sprinklers on the roof and near above-ground fuel tanks. Wet the roof.
- Wet or remove shrubs within 15 feet, or about 4.6 meters, of your residence.
- Gather fire tools such as a rake, axe, handsaw or chainsaw, bucket, and shovel.

- Back your car into the garage or park it in an open space facing the direction of escape. Shut doors and roll up windows. Leave the key in the ignition and the car doors unlocked. Close garage windows and doors, but leave them unlocked. Disconnect automatic garage door openers.
- Open fireplace damper. Close fireplace screens.
- Close windows, vents, doors, blinds or noncombustible window coverings, and heavy drapes. Remove flammable drapes and curtains.
- Move flammable furniture into the center of the residence away from windows and sliding-glass doors.
- Close all interior doors and windows to prevent drafts.
- Place valuables that will not be damaged by water in a pool or pond.

If advised to evacuate, do so immediately. Choose a route away from the fire hazard.

Watch for changes in the speed and direction of the fire and smoke.

After a Wildfire

Do not return to your home until authorities declare conditions safe. Follow the instructions for recovering from a disaster in Chapter 7.

WINTER STORMS AND EXTREME COLD

Heavy snowfall and extreme cold can immobilize an entire region. Even areas that normally experience mild winters can be hit with a major snowstorm or extreme cold. Winter storms can result in flooding, storm surge, closed highways, blocked roads, downed power lines and hypothermia.

Know the Terms

Familiarize yourself with these terms to help identify a winter storm hazard:

Freezing Rain—Rain that freezes when it hits the ground, creating a coating of ice on roads, walkways, trees, and power lines.

Sleet—Rain that turns to ice pellets before reaching the ground. Sleet also causes moisture on roads to freeze and become slippery.

Winter Storm Watch—A winter storm is possible in your area. Tune in to NOAA Weather Radio, commercial radio, or television for more information.

Winter Storm Warning—A winter storm is occurring or will soon occur in your area.

Blizzard Warning—Sustained winds or frequent gusts to 35 mph, or about 56 kph, or greater and considerable amounts of falling or blowing snow (reducing visibility to less than a quarter mile, or about 0.4 km) are expected to prevail for a period of three hours or longer.

Frost/Freeze Warning—Below freezing temperatures are expected.

Winterize your home to extend the life of your fuel supply by insulating walls and attics, caulking and weather-stripping doors and windows, and installing storm windows or covering windows with plastic.

Take Protective Measures

Before Winter Storms and Extreme Cold

Include these items in your disaster supplies kit:

- Rock salt to melt ice on walkways
- Sand to improve traction
- Snow shovels and other snow removal equipment

Prepare for possible isolation in your home by having sufficient heating fuel; regular fuel sources may be cut off. For example, store a good supply of dry, seasoned wood for your fireplace or wood-burning stove.

To winterize your car, do the following:

- Be sure that the battery and ignition system is in top condition and battery terminals clean.
- Ensure antifreeze levels are sufficient to avoid freezing.
- Ensure the heater and defroster work properly.
- Check and repair windshield wiper equipment; ensure proper washer fluid level.
- Ensure the thermostat works properly.
- Check lights and flashing hazard lights for serviceability.
- Check for leaks and crimped pipes in the exhaust system; repair or replace as necessary. Carbon monoxide is deadly and usually gives no warning.
- Check brakes for wear and fluid levels.
- Check oil for level and weight. Heavier oils congeal more at low temperatures and do not lubricate as well.
- Consider snow tires, snow tires with studs, or chains.
- Replace fuel and air filters. Keep water out of the system by using additives and maintaining a full tank of gas.

During a Winter Storm

During a winter storm or under conditions of extreme cold:

- Listen to your radio, television, or NOAA Weather Radio for weather reports and emergency information.

- Eat regularly and drink ample fluids, but avoid caffeine and alcohol.
- Avoid overexertion when shoveling snow. Overexertion can bring on a heart attack—a major cause of death in the winter. If you must shovel snow, stretch before going outside.
- Watch for signs of frostbite. These include loss of feeling and white or pale appearance in extremities such as fingers, toes, ear lobes, and the tip of the nose. If symptoms are detected, get medical help immediately.
- Watch for signs of hypothermia. These include uncontrollable shivering, memory loss, disorientation, incoherence, slurred speech, drowsiness, and apparent exhaustion. If symptoms of hypothermia are detected, get the victim to a warm location, remove wet clothing, warm the center of the body first, and give warm, nonalcoholic beverages if the victim is conscious. Get medical help as soon as possible.
- Conserve fuel, if necessary, by keeping your residence cooler than normal. Temporarily close off heat to some rooms.
- Maintain ventilation when using kerosene heaters to avoid buildup of toxic fumes. Refuel kerosene heaters outside and keep them at least three feet from flammable objects.

Dress for the Weather:

- Wear several layers of loose-fitting, lightweight, warm clothing rather than one layer of heavy clothing. The outer garments should be tightly woven and water repellent.
- Wear mittens, which are warmer than gloves.
- Wear a hat.
- Cover your mouth with a scarf to protect your lungs.

Drive only if it is absolutely necessary. If you must drive, observe these precautions:

- Travel in the day, don't travel alone, and keep others informed of your schedule.
- Stay on main roads; avoid back road shortcuts.

If a blizzard traps you in the car, keep these guidelines in mind:

- Pull off the highway. Turn on hazard lights and hang a distress flag from the radio antenna or window.
- Remain in your vehicle where rescuers are most likely to find you. Do not set out on foot unless you can see a building close by where you know you can take shelter. Be careful; distances are distorted by blowing snow. A building may seem close, but be too far to walk to in deep snow.
- Run the engine and heater about 10 minutes each hour to keep warm. When the engine is running, open an upwind window slightly for ventilation. This will protect you from possible carbon monoxide poisoning. Periodically clear snow from the exhaust pipe.

- Exercise to maintain body heat, but avoid overexertion. In extreme cold, use road maps, seat covers, and floor mats for insulation. Huddle with passengers and use your coat for a blanket.
- Take turns sleeping. One person should be awake at all times to look for rescue crews.
- Drink fluids to avoid dehydration.
- Be careful not to waste battery power. Balance electrical energy needs—the use of lights, heat, and radio—with supply.
- Turn on the inside light at night so work crews or rescuers can see you.
- If stranded in a remote area, stomp large block letters in an open area spelling out H-E-L-P or S-O-S and line with rocks or tree limbs to attract the attention of rescue personnel who may be surveying the area by airplane.
- Leave the car and proceed on foot—if necessary—once the blizzard passes.

After a Winter Storm

Be aware that heavy snow and ice hazards may persist after the snow stops falling. If possible, stay off the roads until the plows have had time to make thoroughfares safe for travel. Follow the instructions for recovering from a disaster in Chapter 7.

PANDEMICS

An influenza (flu) pandemic is a worldwide outbreak of flu disease that occurs when a new type of influenza virus appears that people have not been exposed to before (or have not been exposed to in a long time). People in high-risk groups (particularly people with weakened immune systems, the elderly, and the very young) should get a flu shot every year because flu viruses constantly change. The change is usually very gradual, allowing the public time to build up immunity. Pandemics occur whenever there is a major change in the virus that causes flu. Because people have little or no immunity to the new virus, it can spread rapidly from human to human (by coughing and sneezing) around the world, making many people ill. Pandemics are different from the seasonal outbreaks of influenza that we see every year. Seasonal influenza is caused by influenza virus types to which people have already been exposed. Its impact on society is less severe than a pandemic, and influenza vaccines (flu shots and nasal-spray vaccine) are available to help prevent widespread illness from seasonal flu.

Influenza pandemics are different from many of the other major public health and health care threats facing our country and the world. A pandemic will last much longer than most flu outbreaks and may include so-called waves of influenza activity that last 6–8 weeks separated by a period of several months in between. Health care workers and first responders will also be affected and many will not be able to work. Public health officials will not know how severe a pandemic will be until it begins.

Influenza pandemics are rare but recurring events. In the last century, there were three influenza pandemics (in 1918, 1957, and 1968). They are called pandemics because of their worldwide spread and because they were caused by a new influenza virus. The 1918 pandemic was especially severe, causing up to 50 million deaths worldwide.

Avian Flu

At any given time, there are many different types of influenza viruses circulating around the world. Some of these viruses only infect birds, some only infect swine, and others infect only humans.

The term *bird flu* or *avian influenza* refers to influenza strains that affect birds. One particular avian strain that causes severe illness in birds, named H5N1, has been the subject of widespread media coverage in recent years. Hundreds of millions of chickens and ducks have died or been killed in an effort to control this strain of influenza, yet public health officials have still found the H5N1 virus in birds in many parts of the world. Wild birds are probably spreading the virus, and it can be difficult to detect because infected birds may or may not display symptoms. Domestic poultry is very susceptible to H5N1.

Although the H5N1 virus primarily affects birds, it can also spread to people. Most people who have contracted the virus work directly with poultry or have had close contact with birds. That usually means direct contact with live birds or bird droppings. So far, it does not appear that people can get it easily from each other.

Currently, there is no evidence that H5N1 should be considered a pandemic, but public health experts are concerned that the H5N1 virus could change (mutate) into a form that is easily spread from one person to another. No one knows for sure whether that will happen, or when it might happen. If the H5N1 virus does change into a human communicable strain, it could result in a global influenza pandemic. Since few, if any, people would have any immunity to the new influenza virus, it could spread around the world very rapidly, causing serious illness in many people.

Humans are infected by H5N1 through direct contact with infected birds or surfaces and objects contaminated by their feces. To date (2006), most human cases have occurred in areas where many households keep small poultry flocks, which often roam freely, sometimes entering homes or sharing outdoor areas where children play. Because infected birds shed large quantities of virus in their feces, there are multiple opportunities for human exposure to infected droppings or to environments contaminated by the virus in these settings. More than 250 human cases have been laboratory confirmed in Cambodia, Indonesia, Thailand, Vietnam, Mongolia, China, Turkey, Russia, Romania, Greece, Egypt, Iraq, Azerbaijan, and Djibouti. More than half of these people have died. Possible cases of the virus have also been found in Croatia, Bulgaria, and in the United Kingdom. Unlike more common seasonal influenza, most cases have occurred in previously healthy children and young adults.

It is important to note that it is safe to eat properly cooked poultry. Cooking destroys germs, including bird flu viruses. The United States maintains trade restrictions on the importation of poultry and poultry products from countries where the highly pathogenic H5N1 avian influenza strain has been detected in commercial or traditionally raised poultry. To safely prepare poultry, observe these guidelines:

- Wash hands before and after handling food.
- Keep raw poultry and its juices away from other foods.
- Keep hands, utensils, and surfaces, such as cutting boards, clean (wash cutting boards after preparing poultry and before reusing for other foods).
- Use a food thermometer to ensure that food has reached the safe internal temperature in all parts of the bird. Cook poultry to at least 165°F, or 74°C, to kill food-borne germs that might be present, including the avian influenza virus.

SARS

SARS-CoV is a highly contagious form of atypical pneumonia caused by a coronavirus that has the potential to become pandemic. Rapid action by national and international health authorities such as the World Health Organization helped slow transmission and eventually broke the chain of transmission, ending the localized epidemics before they could become a pandemic. However, the disease has not been eradicated and it could reemerge unexpectedly. Public health officials recommend that physicians report all cases of atypical pneumonia.

Superbugs

Antibiotic-resistant superbugs may also revive diseases that have been all but eradicated. Cases of tuberculosis resistant to all traditionally effective treatments have emerged. Such common bacteria as *Staphylococcus aureus, Serratia marcescens,* and species of *Enterococcus* that have developed resistance to the strongest available antibiotics, such as Vancomycin, emerged in the past 20 years as an important cause of hospital-acquired nosocomial infections and are now colonizing and causing disease in the general population. The condition is rare but in some cases antibiotic-resistant Group A streptococcus can cause flesh-eating bacteria (necrotizing fasciitis), an infection of the deeper layers of skin.

HIV

HIV (Human Immunodeficiency Virus), the virus that causes AIDS (Acquired Immunodeficiency Syndrome), is now considered a global pandemic with infection rates as high as 25 percent in southern and eastern Africa. Infection with HIV occurs by the transfer of blood, semen, vaginal fluid, Cowper's fluid, or breast milk. Effective education about safer sexual practices and blood-borne infection precautions training have helped to slow down infection rates in several African countries sponsoring national education programs. Infection rates are rising again in Asia and the Americas.

Other Exotic Threats

Lassa fever, Rift Valley fever, Marburg virus, Ebola virus, and Bolivian hemorrhagic fever are highly contagious and deadly diseases with the theoretical potential to become pandemics. Their ability to spread efficiently enough to cause a pandemic is limited because transmission of these viruses requires close contact with the infected vector. Genetic mutations could occur at which could elevate their potential for causing widespread harm.

Vaccines

Vaccines are used to protect people from contracting a virus once a particular threat is identified and they are generally considered the first line of defense. After an individual has been infected by a virus, a vaccine generally cannot help to fight it. Because viruses change over time, a specific pandemic influenza vaccine cannot be produced until a pandemic influenza virus emerges and is identified. Once a pandemic influenza virus has been identified, it will likely take several months to develop, test, and begin producing a vaccine.

While there is currently no human pandemic influenza in the world, the federal government is facilitating production of vaccines for several existing avian influenza viruses. These vaccines may provide some protection should one of these viruses change and cause an influenza pandemic. The supply of pandemic vaccine will be limited, particularly in the early stages of a pandemic. Efforts are being made to increase vaccine-manufacturing capacity in the United States so that supplies of vaccines would be more readily available. In addition, research is underway to develop new ways to produce vaccines more quickly.

Because people will have had no prior exposure to a pandemic strain of influenza, everyone will need two doses: a primer and then a booster about four weeks later. So even those first in line for vaccines are unlikely to develop immunity until at least several months following the start of a pandemic.

Antivirals

A number of antiviral drugs are approved by the U.S. Food and Drug Administration to treat and prevent seasonal influenza. Some of these antiviral medications may be effective in treating pandemic influenza. These drugs may help prevent infection in people at risk and shorten the duration of symptoms in those infected with pandemic influenza. However, it is unlikely that antiviral medications alone would effectively contain the spread of pandemic influenza. The federal government is stockpiling antiviral medications that would most likely be used in the early stages of an influenza pandemic and working to develop new antiviral medications. These drugs are available by prescription only.

Antiviral drugs that fight the virus directly are the optimal treatment, but many H5N1 patients have arrived on doctors' doorsteps too late for the drugs to do much good. The version of the strain that has infected most human victims is also resistant to an older class of antivirals called amantadines, possibly as a result of those drugs having been given to poultry in parts of Asia. Laboratory experiments indicate that H5N1 is still susceptible to a newer class of antivirals called neuraminidase inhibitors (NI) that includes two products, oseltamivir and zanamivir, currently on the market under the brand names Tamiflu and Relenza. The former comes in pill form; the latter is a powder delivered by inhaler. To be effective against seasonal flu strains, either drug must be taken within 48 hours of symptoms appearing.

Know the Terms

Familiarize yourself with these terms to stay informed so that you can prepare yourself and your family:

Pandemic—An epidemic (an outbreak of a human to human infectious disease) that spreads worldwide, or at least across a large region. Pandemics occur whenever a virus enters the population that can easily spread from human to human and people have little or no immunity to it.

Avian Flu—Avian influenza, or bird flu, refers to a large group of different influenza viruses that primarily affect birds. On rare occasions, these bird viruses can infect other species, including pigs and humans. The vast majority of avian influenza viruses do not infect humans. An influenza pandemic happens when a new subtype emerges that has not previously circulated in humans.

H5N1—Influenza A virus subtype H5N1, also known as A(H5N1), is a subtype of the Influenza A virus that can cause illness in humans and many other animal species including birds. A bird-adapted strain of H5N1 is commonly known as avian influenza or bird flu.

SARS—SARS-CoV is a highly contagious form of atypical pneumonia caused by a coronavirus that has the potential to become pandemic.

HIV—Human Immunodeficiency Virus is a retrovirus that causes Acquired Immunodeficiency Syndrome (AIDS), a condition in which the immune system begins to fail, leading to life-threatening opportunistic infections. Previous names for the virus include Human T-Lymphotropic Virus-III (HTLV-III) and lymphadenopathy-associated virus (LAV). Infection with HIV occurs by the transfer of blood, semen, vaginal fluid, Cowper's fluid, or breast milk.

Ebola—The common term for a group of viruses belonging to genus *Ebolavirus*, which cause Ebola hemorrhagic fever. The disease can be deadly and encompasses a range of symptoms, usually including vomiting, diarrhea, general body pain, internal and external bleeding, and fever. Mortality rates are generally high, ranging from 50 to 90 percent.

Vaccines—A vaccine is an antigenic preparation used to establish immunity to a disease. Because viruses change over time, a specific pandemic influenza vaccine cannot be produced until a pandemic influenza virus emerges and is identified. The supply of pandemic vaccine will be limited, particularly in the early stages of a pandemic. Because people will have had no prior exposure to a pandemic strain of influenza, everyone will need two doses: a primer and then a booster about four weeks later. So even those first in line for vaccines are unlikely to develop immunity until at least several months following the start of a pandemic.

Antivirals—Antiviral drugs are a class of medication used specifically for treating viral infections. Like antibiotics, specific antivirals are used for specific viruses. Antiviral drugs are one class of antimicrobials, a larger group that also includes antibiotics, antifungal and antiparasitic drugs. They are relatively harmless to the host and therefore can be used to treat infections. Laboratory experiments indicate that H5N1 is still susceptible to a newer class of antivirals called neuraminidase inhibitors (NI) that includes two products, oseltamivir and zanamivir, currently on the market under the brand names Tamiflu and Relenza. The former comes in pill form; the latter is a powder delivered by inhaler. To be effective against seasonal flu strains, either drug must be taken within 48 hours of symptoms appearing.

Quarantine—A quarantine is enforced isolation, typically to contain the spread of a dangerous disease.

NIOSH—The National Institute for Occupational Safety and Health (NIOSH) is the federal agency responsible for conducting research and making recommendations for the prevention of work-related injury and illness. NIOSH is part of the Centers for Disease Control and Prevention (CDC) in the Department of Health and Human Services.

N95—An N95 respirator is a particulate respirator or air-purifying respirator. It provides protection by filtering particles out of the air you breathe (at least 95 percent of airborne particles). Workers can wear any one of the particulate respirators for protection against diseases spread through the air if they are NIOSH approved and if they have been properly fit tested and maintained.

Take Protective Measures

Before a Pandemic

When a pandemic starts, everyone around the world could be at risk and many people will die. All of our day-to-day lives will change. Authorities may place restrictions on travel and public gatherings to slow the spread of the virus and people might have to stay home from work or school for an extended period of time. Essential services including public utilities and medical care will be undermanned and medicines will be in short supply.

You can reduce the effects of a pandemic on your family if you prepare ahead of time.

To prepare for a pandemic threat, take the following precautions:

- Check with your doctor to ensure that all required or suggested immunizations are up to date. Children and older adults may be particularly vulnerable to some pandemic threats (to some degree, this was the case in 1957 and 1968). Plan to get your annual influenza vaccination to help boost your immune system (the seasonal flu shot will not protect you against pandemic influenza but it will help you to avoid the seasonal flu to stay healthy and strong). If you are over the age of 65 or have a chronic illness such as diabetes or asthma, get a pneumonia shot to prevent secondary infection.
- Have your disaster supplies kit on hand with medical supplies and at a minimum a 72 hour (3 day) supply of food and water for all people and pets in your household (1 gallon, or about 4 liters, of water per person, per day). Ideally, you should prepare for a two week stay at home.
- In case banks are closed or automatic teller machines are shut down, keep cash or traveler's checks in small denominations in a safe place at home.
- Stay informed and up to date. Check the World Health Organization (WHO), Pandemic Influenza, and Center for Disease Control (CDC) Websites (refer to Chapter 3 for a list of resources), read articles from trusted sources, watch the news, and listen to the radio.
- Do not handle, play with, or pick up dead birds (or other animals).
- Teach your children good hygiene (and model that behavior) to protect them from the influenza virus (and other contagious diseases):
  - Wash your hands frequently before eating and after using the washroom.
  - Always avoid touching your eyes, nose, or mouth.
  - When you are sick, stay home to stop the spread of infection.
  - Teach your children to stay away from others who are sick.
  - Cover your cough and sneeze with your upper sleeve or use a tissue (then throw it away immediately).

- Keep an alcohol-based, waterless hand cleaner handy for times when you don't have access to soap and water.
- To boost your immune system, practice a healthy lifestyle by eating healthy foods, exercising regularly, and getting enough sleep.
- Teach your family about the basics of pandemic influenza.
- Develop your own family plan for a pandemic so that you can address issues such as family illness and work, school, or day-care closures.
- Designate an out-of-town relative or friend to act as a common contact for your family members.
- Make a list of phone numbers of hospitals, doctors (including Pediatricians), pharmacies, and health units. Place them near the phone or on your fridge and in your wallet/pocketbook. Let family members know where these numbers are located. Include a list of allergies for each family member.

- Store emergency numbers in your cell phones under "ICE" (In Case of Emergency), so that someone else can call your emergency numbers if you are incapacitated.

- Know what routes you will use if you must evacuate (plan multiple routes in case major highways are congested or blocked). Be aware that you may have to contend with fuel shortages and keep a full gas can in your garage.

- Have a financial plan in case you or a family member is unable to work for a period of time due to illness or family illness.

- Have enough prescription medicines on hand for at least six weeks.

- Stock over-the-counter medications, such as acetaminophen, ibuprofen or Aspirin®, antacid and cough/cold medication. Aspirin® should not be given to children 20 years or younger because of the risk of Reye's Syndrome.

- If you receive ongoing medical care such as dialysis, chemotherapy, or other therapies, talk with your health care provider about plans to continue care during a pandemic.

- Find out what your own community is doing to prepare for a pandemic. Ask your local government, school district, parent-teacher organizations, day care, your employer, public health agencies, emergency response units, voluntary organizations, and churches about their preparations for a pandemic. Find out where you fit in and how you can help.

- If you can, make arrangements to work from home (telecommute) during a pandemic. If you must work in the office, limit your face-to-face interaction with others and hold meetings using teleconferencing facilities. Ask your employer to consider using staggered work schedules and modifying the office layout or seating arrangements.

- Consider keeping your children home from school during a pandemic. Identify strategies for providing education services to students during a school closure, including the Web, phone trees, mailed lessons and assignments, radio, and television.

- Have games, reading material, and other entertainment items available for children and adults. You might need to stay at home for an extended period of time during a pandemic.

- If you must travel, check travel advisories and know where the pandemic threat is most prevalent.

- If you have been traveling in areas where influenza activity is high, monitor your health (watch for symptoms of fever and cough). If you experience any symptoms, call your doctor immediately.

- If you own a business, make sure you have a plan in place to address employee absenteeism and a possible decrease in sales and revenue.

- Talk with neighbors, seniors and others in your neighborhood to see if they are preparing for a pandemic, and if they will require any help. Pool your resources.

- If you know a health care worker, emergency responder or other frontline workers, talk with them now to find out how you can help them during a pandemic.

- Review and revise your disaster plans regularly and rotate stored food and water supplies.

- Consider installing a High Efficiency Particulate Air (HEPA) filter in your furnace return duct. These filters remove particles in the 0.3 to 10 micron range and will filter out most biological agents that may enter your house. If you do not have a central heating or cooling system, consider using a stand-alone portable HEPA filter. These filters remove dust, vapors, bacteria and fungi. HEPA filters also effectively capture some viruses.

- Consider purchasing fit-tested N95 or higher respirators or powered air-purifying respirators (PAPR) for your family members.

During a Pandemic

In some situations, people may be alerted to potential exposure. If this is the case, pay close attention to all official warnings and instructions about how to proceed. The delivery of medical services for a pandemic outbreak may be handled differently to respond to increased demand. The basic public health procedures and medical protocols for handling exposure to pandemics are the same as for any infectious disease.

In the event of a pandemic outbreak, public health officials may not immediately be able to provide information about what you should do. It will take time to determine what the illness is, how it should be treated, and who is in danger. Watch television, listen to radio, check the Internet, and monitor emergency alert systems for official news and information, including signs and symptoms of the disease; areas in danger; whether medications, vaccinations, or antivirals are being distributed; and where you should seek medical attention if you become ill.

Be suspicious of any symptoms you notice, but do not assume that any illness is a result of the pandemic. Use common sense and practice good hygiene.

Once public health officials determine the specific nature of a pandemic outbreak, authorities may put special measures in place to contain the threat, such as banning public gatherings or shutting down mass transit. If children are especially susceptible to the virus, or if they are found to be an important source of community spread, then governments may consider closing schools.

If a pandemic outbreak occurs in your area, follow these guidelines:

- Avoid public gatherings and places like shopping malls and mass-transit facilities.
- Routinely wash with soap and water. Some level of paranoia is warranted. Avoid touching your eyes, nose, or mouth.
- Listen to the media and public health information outlets for official instructions. Check the World Health Organization (WHO), Pandemic Influenza, and Center for Disease Control (CDC) Websites for current information (refer to Chapter 3 for a list of resources).
- Symptoms of an influenza pandemic in humans may include typical seasonal influenza-like symptoms (fever, cough, sore throat, and muscle aches), eye infections, pneumonia, severe respiratory diseases (such as acute respiratory distress syndrome), and other severe and life-threatening complications. Seek medical attention if you or a member of your family becomes sick.
- Do not handle, play with, or pick up dead birds (or other animals).
- Carry an alcohol-based, waterless hand cleaner and use it frequently.

- Maintain your immune system by eating healthy foods and getting enough sleep.
- Heed instructions to evacuate (be prepared to use alternate routes in case major highways are congested or blocked).
- Refill prescription medicines promptly at the first signs of a pandemic outbreak (maintain at least six weeks' supply).
- At the first signs of a pandemic outbreak, stock up on over-the-counter medications, such as acetaminophen, ibuprofen or Aspirin®, antacid and cough/cold medication. Aspirin® should not be given to children 20 years or younger because of the risk of Reye's Syndrome.
- If you receive ongoing medical care such as dialysis, chemotherapy, or other therapies, confirm the availability of these services with your health care provider.
- Contact your local government, school district, parent-teacher organizations, daycare, your employer, public health agencies, emergency response units, voluntary organizations, and churches about their relief services.
- If you can, work from home (telecommute). If you must work in the office, limit your face-to-face interaction with others and hold meetings using teleconferencing facilities.
- Consider keeping your children home from school. Use alternate education services including the Web, phone trees, mailed lessons and assignments, radio, and television.
- Avoid travel.
- Talk with neighbors, seniors and others in your neighborhood to see if they require any help. Pool your resources. Do not take any unnecessary risks and take measures protect your family first.
- If you know a health care worker, emergency responder or other frontline workers, contact them to get current information.
- Use a High Efficiency Particulate Air (HEPA) filter or air purifier in your home.
- If you are a first responder, place surgical masks on patients to contain droplets expelled during coughing. If this is not possible, have the patient cover mouth/nose with tissue when coughing or use another practical method to contain cough.
- If you are a first responder, wear a fit-tested N95 or higher respirator or powered air-purifying respirator (PAPR) during close contact with and transport of patients. If respirators are not available, you can wear a tightly fitting surgical mask, but it will offer significantly less protection than a respirator. Although N95 respirators can be reused in the care of tuberculosis (TB) patients, you should not reuse them after during the ongoing care of avian influenza patients since, unlike TB, influenza can also be transmitted by contact. You should discard N95 respirators in biohazard bags after caring for a patient (between patients) or when soiled or damaged.
- If you must transport an infected patient, keep the windows of your vehicle open (if feasible) and set the heating and air-conditioning systems on a nonrecirculating cycle.
- If you are a first responder, wear long-sleeved fluid-resistant Personal Protective Equipment (PPE), eye protection, and disposable gloves. Note that you should

always wash your hands with antimicrobial soap and water or an alcohol-based hand cleaner immediately upon removing your gloves.

The experts recommended surgical masks for flu patients and health workers exposed to those patients. For healthy people, hand washing offers more protection than wearing masks in public, because people can be exposed to the virus at home, at work and by touching contaminated surfaces (including the surface of a mask).

After a Pandemic Outbreak

Be prepared for successive outbreaks. A pandemic will last much longer than most flu outbreaks and may include "waves" of influenza activity that last 6–8 weeks separated by a period of several months in between.

A true pandemic will affect all of us. Be prepared to address the special emotional needs of children in the aftermath. Follow the instructions for recovering from a disaster in Chapter 7.

OTHER DISEASE THREATS

Lyme Disease

Lyme disease is a bacterial infection commonly transmitted by infected deer ticks that typically feed on small mammals, birds and deer but may also feed on cats, dogs, and humans. Although the disease has been reported in nearly all states, most cases are concentrated in the Mid-Atlantic and northeast states. A number of cases also have been reported in Wisconsin, Minnesota, and northern California.

Most people who are infected have a circular, red rash surrounding the site of a tick bite; swelling in their joints; and, sometimes, facial paralysis.

West Nile Virus

West Nile virus can affect humans, birds, mosquitoes, and some other animals. Until 1999, the virus was only common in Africa, West Asia, and the Middle East. The first case of West Nile virus was reported in the United States in the early summer of 1999. Signs of the severe form of the infection include headache, high fever, neck stiffness, stupor, disorientation, tremors, coma, convulsions, muscle weakness, and paralysis. Everybody is at risk for getting infected with West Nile virus, but certain people are more likely to get sick from it than others. People over the age of 50 are at the highest risk for developing the severe form of the disease. While many people believe that only those in poor health have to worry about West Nile virus, healthy, active adults who spend much of their time outdoors are at increased risk. Relatively few children get the severe form of the disease.

Take Protective Measures

Lyme Disease

To protect yourself from contracting Lyme disease, take these precautions:

- Avoid tick-infested areas, if you can.
- If you do venture out, stick to paths and avoid walking or hiking through uncleared woodlands, shrubs, bushes, and grassy areas next to woodlands.
- Wear protective, light-colored clothing that minimizes exposed skin and provides a contrast to ticks, making them more visible. Tuck your pant legs into your socks, and tuck your shirt into your pants.
- Use tick and insect repellents, and apply them to your exposed skin or clothing, following directions on product labels. Insect repellents that contain DEET are generally the most effective (again, be careful to follow the manufacturer's directions).
- If you are outdoors and may have been exposed to ticks, check your entire body every day to locate and remove ticks, especially at the end of the day. If you remove attached ticks from a family member, you should monitor them closely for signs and symptoms of tick-borne diseases for up to 30 days. Single-dose doxycycline therapy may be considered for deer tick bites when the tick has been on the person for at least 36 hours.
- Brush off your clothing and your pets' coats before going indoors so that you do not bring unattached ticks into the house.
- Check children's skin thoroughly, including skin folds and the head, scalp, and neck area.
- When ticks attach to the skin, promptly remove them to greatly reduce the chance of infection. The best method for removal is to grasp the tick as close to the skin as possible with thin tweezers and gently pull straight up. Do not attempt to remove ticks by applying heat or other agents.
- If you do remove an attached tick, save it and bring it to your health care provider within 72 hrs of removal to discuss whether single-dose antibiotic prophylaxis (prevention) may be warranted.

West Nile Virus

In most areas, the majority of severe cases occur in the late summer and early fall. But the virus can be transmitted year-round in southern climates where the temperatures are milder.

The most common way humans get West Nile virus is from a bite by an infected mosquito. The good news is that approximately 80 percent of people who are infected with the virus don't even get sick. About 20 percent will experience mild, flulike symptoms, but 1 out of every 150 infected people will develop a more severe illness, which can result in coma, paralysis, and even death.

To protect yourself from contracting West Nile Virus, take these precautions:

- Use tick and insect repellents and apply them to your exposed skin or clothing, following directions on product labels. Insect repellents that contain DEET are generally the most effective (again, be careful to follow the manufacturer's directions). Products containing 10 percent or less DEET are the most appropriate for children aged 2–12 years. Pet owners should not use human repellents that contain DEET on animals.

- Be sure to protect yourself or limit your time outdoors when mosquitoes are most active, from dusk to dawn.
- Reduce the number of mosquitoes around your home by getting rid of standing water (check outside for water left in unused containers, flowerpots, birdbaths, and pool covers). Clean out clogged rain gutters to avoid collecting water where mosquitoes can lay eggs.
- Maintain your window and door screens to keep the mosquitoes outside.
- West Nile virus can infect your pets and horses, but it rarely causes illnesses in domestic pets. A USDA-licensed equine vaccine for the virus is now available through veterinarians. Pet owners should not use human repellents that contain DEET on animals. Check with your veterinarian for the appropriate products to protect your pet. Also contact your veterinarian if your pet shows signs of infection including fever, depression, lack of coordination, muscle weakness or spasms, or seizures or paralysis.
- Contact your municipal authorities to recommend that they take mosquito control measures during the summer months.
- Be advised that it is important to always practice prevention, even if your community employs mosquito control measures. The control activities cannot kill every mosquito.

If You Suspect that You Might Be Infected

Lyme Disease

The most common sign of Lyme disease is a characteristic rash called erythema migrans. Usually, it appears as an expanding red ring surrounding the site of a tick bite, although many people may not be aware they were bitten. Other symptoms may include arthritis, meningitis, and facial paralysis. Be advised that a person may have Lyme disease without presenting the most obvious symptoms. A tick bite can also transmit more than one tick-borne illness, further complicating Lyme disease diagnosis and treatment.

- If you experience the noted symptoms (especially a circular red rash around the site of a tick bite) after removing a tick or visiting tick-infested areas, you should promptly seek medical attention.
- If not treated early, people with Lyme disease may develop late symptoms such as meningitis, numbness, tingling or burning sensations in the extremities, arthritis, and an abnormally slow heart rate. If you experience these symptoms and the cause is not immediately apparent, you should promptly seek medical attention. Delayed diagnosis and treatment can lead to serious brain, heart, or joint problems.
- Lyme disease is usually diagnosed by the presence of a characteristic rash and a history of recent tick exposure. If you experience only nonrash manifestations,

consult with your doctor to initiate laboratory tests used to support the diagnosis and to rule out other possible diagnoses.

- Most patients who develop Lyme disease are cured with a single course of 14–28 days of antibiotics, depending on the stage of their illness. Occasionally a second course of treatment is necessary. More prolonged antibiotic therapy is not recommended and may be dangerous.

- Patients who continue to have symptoms that persist after appropriate antibiotic treatment for Lyme disease should consult their physicians about whether the diagnosis was accurate or if they may have a different or new illness.

West Nile Virus

Currently, there is no vaccine or specific treatment for West Nile virus infection. The most important thing that you can do is to limit your exposure to mosquito bites.

Symptoms of a West Nile virus illness usually develop within two weeks (the incubation period) after the mosquito bite, if at all (about 80 percent of cases are asymptomatic). The mild form of the illness is accompanied with fever, headaches, body aches, and, occasionally, a skin rash on the trunk of the body and swollen lymph glands. These symptoms usually last only a few days and leave no permanent damage.

If you are concerned that you or a family member might have contracted West Nile virus, you should see your doctor immediately. A health professional can assess your situation and, if necessary, test for and/or treat the infection. Although there is no cure for the disease, your doctor can treat the symptoms while your body fights infection from West Nile virus.

CHAPTER 5

Technological Hazards

Technological hazards include hazardous materials incidents and nuclear power plant failures. Usually, little or no warning precedes incidents involving technological hazards. In many cases, victims may not know they have been affected until many years later. For example, health problems caused by hidden toxic waste sites—like that at Love Canal, near Niagara Falls, New York—surfaced years after initial exposure. The number of technological incidents is escalating, mainly as a result of the increased number of new substances and the opportunities for human error inherent in the use of these materials.

Use this chapter to learn what actions to include in your family disaster plan to prepare for and respond to events involving technological hazards. Learn how to use, store, and dispose of household chemicals in a manner that will reduce the potential for injury to people and the environment. When you complete this chapter, you will be able to do the following:

- Recognize important terms.
- Take protective measures for technological disasters.
- Know what actions to take if an event occurs.
- Identify resources for more information about technological hazards.

HAZARDOUS MATERIALS INCIDENTS

Chemicals are found everywhere. They are used to purify drinking water, increase crop production, and simplify household chores. But chemicals also can be hazardous to humans or the environment if used or released improperly.

Hazards can occur during production, storage, transportation, use, or disposal. You and your community are at risk if a chemical is used unsafely or released in harmful amounts into the environment where you live, work, or play. Chemical manufacturers are one source of hazardous materials, but there are many others, including service stations, hospitals, and hazardous materials waste sites.

Take Protective Measures

Before a Hazardous Materials Incident

Many communities have Local Emergency Planning Committees (LEPCs) whose responsibilities include collecting information about hazardous materials in the community and making this information available to the public upon request. The LEPCs also are tasked with developing an emergency plan to prepare for and respond to chemical emergencies in the community. Ways the public will be notified and actions the public must take in the event of a release are part of the plan. Contact the LEPCs to find out more about chemical hazards and what needs to be done to minimize the risk to individuals and the community from these materials. The local emergency management office can provide contact information for the LEPCs.

To prepare for a hazardous materials incident, include these items in your disaster supplies kit:

- Plastic sheeting (10 mil, or 0.01 inch or about 0.25 mm, thickness)
- Duct tape
- Scissors

During a Hazardous Materials Incident

Listen to local radio or television stations for detailed information and instructions. Follow the instructions carefully. You should stay away from the area to minimize the risk of contamination. Remember that some toxic chemicals are odorless.

- **If Authorities Instruct You to Evacuate**—Leave immediately. *Do not* second-guess the instruction or seek out confirmation.
- **If You Are Outside**—Stay upstream, uphill, and upwind! In general, try to go at least one-half mile (usually 8–10 city blocks) from the danger area. Do not walk into or touch any spilled liquids, airborne mists, or condensed solid chemical deposits.
- **If You Are in a Vehicle**—Stop and seek shelter in a permanent building. If you must remain in your car, keep car windows and vents closed, and shut off the air conditioner and heater.
- **If Authorities Instruct You to Shelter in Place (or Stay Indoors)**—Close and lock all exterior doors and windows. Close vents, fireplace dampers, and as many interior doors as possible.

- Turn off air conditioners and ventilation systems to prevent drawing outside air into the building.
- Go into the preselected shelter room. This room should be above ground and have the fewest openings to the outside.
- Seal the room by covering each window, door, and vent using plastic sheeting and duct tape. Fill all cracks and holes (including spaces around pipes and cracks under doorways).

Shelter Safety for Sealed Rooms

Ten square feet, or about one square meter, of floor space per person will provide sufficient air to prevent carbon dioxide build-up for up to five hours, assuming a normal breathing rate while resting. However, local officials are unlikely to recommend the public shelter in a sealed room for more than 2–3 hours because the effectiveness of such sheltering diminishes with time as the contaminated outside air gradually seeps into the shelter. At this point, evacuation from the area is the better protective action to take. In addition, you should ventilate the shelter when the emergency has passed to avoid breathing contaminated air still inside the shelter.

After a Hazardous Materials Incident

Following a hazardous materials incident, do the following:

- Return home only when authorities say it is safe to do so. Open windows and vents, and turn on fans to provide ventilation.
- Act quickly if you have come in to contact with or have been exposed to hazardous chemicals:
  - Follow decontamination instructions from local authorities. You may be advised to take a thorough shower, or you may be advised to stay away from water and follow another procedure.
  - Seek medical treatment for unusual symptoms as soon as possible.
  - Place exposed clothing and shoes in tightly sealed containers. Do not allow them to contact other materials. Call local authorities to find out about proper disposal.
  - Advise everyone who comes in to contact with you that you may have been exposed to a toxic substance.
- Find out from local authorities how to clean up your land and property.
- Report any lingering vapors or other hazards to your local emergency services office.
- Follow the instructions for recovering from a disaster in Chapter 7.

HOUSEHOLD CHEMICAL EMERGENCIES

Nearly every household uses products containing hazardous materials or chemicals. Typical household hazardous materials and chemicals are listed below.

Cleaning Products

- Oven cleaners
- Drain cleaners
- Wood and metal cleaners and polishes
- Toilet cleaners
- Tub, tile, and shower cleaners
- Bleach (laundry)
- Pool chemicals

Indoor Pesticides

- Ant sprays and baits
- Cockroach sprays and baits
- Flea repellents and shampoos
- Bug sprays
- Houseplant insecticides
- Moth repellents
- Mouse and rat poisons and baits

Lawn and Garden Products

- Herbicides
- Insecticides
- Fungicides/wood preservatives

Workshop Supplies

- Adhesives and glues
- Furniture strippers
- Paints
- Stains and varnishes
- Paint thinners and turpentine
- Paint strippers and removers
- Photographic chemicals
- Fixatives and other solvents

Automotive Products

- Gasoline
- Motor oil
- Fuel additives

- Carburetor and fuel-injection cleaners
- Air-conditioning refrigerants
- Starter fluids
- Automotive batteries
- Transmission and brake fluid
- Antifreeze

Flammable Products

- Propane tanks
- Kerosene
- Home heating oil
- Diesel fuel
- Gas/oil mixtures
- Lighter fluid

Miscellaneous Materials

- Batteries
- Mercury thermostats or thermometers
- Fluorescent light bulbs
- Driveway sealer

Although the risk of a chemical accident is slight, knowing how to handle these products and how to react during an emergency can reduce the risk of injury.

Take Protective Measures

Before a Household Chemical Emergency

How to buy and store hazardous household chemicals safely is outlined below:

- Buy only as much of a chemical as you think you will use. Leftover material can be shared with neighbors or donated to a business, charity, or government agency. For example, excess pesticide could be offered to a greenhouse or garden center, and theater groups often need surplus paint. Some communities have organized waste exchanges where household hazardous chemicals and waste can be swapped or given away.
- Keep products containing hazardous materials in their original containers, and never remove the labels unless the container is corroding. Corroding containers should be repackaged and clearly labeled.
- Never store hazardous products in food containers.

- Never mix household hazardous chemicals or waste with other products. Incompatibles, such as chlorine bleach and ammonia, may react, ignite, or explode.

To prevent and respond to accidents, follow these guidelines:

- Follow the manufacturer's instructions for the proper use of the household chemical.
- Never smoke while using household chemicals.
- Never use hair spray, cleaning solutions, paint products, or pesticides near an open flame (e.g., pilot light, lighted candle, fireplace, wood burning stove, etc.). Although you may not be able to see or smell them, vapor particles in the air could catch fire or explode.
- Clean up any chemical spill immediately. Use rags to clean up the spill. Wear gloves and eye protection. Allow the fumes in the rags to evaporate outdoors, then dispose of the rags by wrapping them in a newspaper and placing them in a sealed plastic bag in your trash can.
- Dispose of hazardous materials correctly. Take household hazardous waste to a local collection program. Check with your county or state environmental or solid waste agency to learn if there is a household hazardous waste collection program in your area.

Learn to recognize the symptoms of toxic poisoning, which are as follows:

- Difficulty breathing
- Irritation of the eyes, skin, throat, or respiratory tract
- Changes in skin color
- Headache or blurred vision
- Dizziness
- Clumsiness or lack of coordination
- Cramps or diarrhea

Be prepared to seek medical assistance:

- Post the number of the emergency medical services and the poison control center by all telephones. In an emergency situation, you may not have time to look up critical phone numbers. The national poison control number is (800) 222-1222.

During a Household Chemical Emergency

If there is a danger of fire or explosion, do the following:

- Get out of the residence immediately. Do not waste time collecting items or calling the fire department when you are in danger. Call the fire department from outside (a cellular phone or a neighbor's phone) once you are safely away from danger.
- Stay upwind and away from the residence to avoid breathing toxic fumes.

If someone has been exposed to a household chemical, follow these guidelines:

• Find any containers of the substance that are readily available in order to provide requested information to emergency responders. Call emergency medical services.
• Follow the emergency operator or dispatcher's first-aid instructions carefully. The first-aid advice found on containers may be out of date or inappropriate. Do not give anything by mouth unless advised to do so by a medical professional.

Discard clothing that may have been contaminated. Some chemicals may not wash out completely.

Checking Your Home

There are probably many hazardous materials throughout your home. Take a tour of your home to see where these materials are located. Use the list of common hazardous household items presented earlier to guide you in your hunt. Once you have located a product, check the label and take the necessary steps to ensure that you are using, storing, and disposing of the material according to the manufacturer's directions. It is critical to store household chemicals in places where children cannot access them. Remember that products such as aerosol cans of hair spray and deodorant, nail polish and nail polish remover, toilet bowl cleaners, and furniture polishes all fall into the category of hazardous materials.

NUCLEAR POWER PLANT EMERGENCIES

Nuclear power plants use the heat generated from nuclear fission in a contained environment to convert water to steam, which powers generators to produce electricity. Nuclear power plants operate in most states in the country and produce about 20 percent of the nation's power. Nearly 3 million Americans live within 10 miles, or about 16 km, of an operating nuclear power plant.

Although the construction and operation of these facilities are closely monitored and regulated by the Nuclear Regulatory Commission (NRC), accidents are possible. An accident could result in dangerous levels of radiation that could affect the health and safety of the public living near the nuclear power plant.

Local and state governments, federal agencies, and the electric utilities have emergency response plans in the event of a nuclear power plant incident. The plans define two emergency planning zones. One zone covers an area within a 10-mile, or about a 16 km, radius of the plant where it is possible that people could be harmed by direct radiation exposure. The second zone covers a broader area, usually up to a 50-mile, or about an 80 km, radius from the plant, where radioactive materials could contaminate water supplies, food crops, and livestock.

The potential danger from an accident at a nuclear power plant is exposure to radiation. This exposure could come from the release of radioactive material from the plant into the environment, usually characterized by a plume (cloudlike formation) of radioactive gases and particles. The major hazards to people in the vicinity of the plume are radiation exposure from the cloud and particles deposited on the ground, inhalation of radioactive materials, and ingestion of radioactive materials.

Radioactive materials are composed of atoms that are unstable. An unstable atom gives off its excess energy until it becomes stable. The energy emitted is radiation. Each of us is exposed to radiation daily from natural sources, including the sun and the earth. Small traces of radiation are present in food and water. Radiation is also released from man-made sources such as X-ray machines, television sets, and microwave ovens. Radiation has a cumulative effect. The longer a person is exposed to radiation, the greater the effect. A high exposure to radiation can cause serious illness or death.

Minimizing Exposure to Radiation

- **Distance**—The more distance between you and the source of the radiation, the better. This could mean evacuation or remaining indoors to minimize exposure.
- **Shielding**—The more heavy, dense material between you and the source of the radiation, the better.
- **Time**—Most radioactivity loses its strength fairly quickly.

If an accident at a nuclear power plant were to release radiation in your area, local authorities would activate warning sirens or another approved alert method. They also would instruct you through the Emergency Alert System (EAS) on local television and radio stations on how to protect yourself.

Know the Terms

Familiarize yourself with these terms to help identify a nuclear power plant emergency:

Notification of Unusual Event—A small problem has occurred at the plant. No radiation leak is expected. No action on your part will be necessary.

Alert—A small problem has occurred, and small amounts of radiation could leak inside the plant. This will not affect you, and no action is required.

Site Area Emergency—Area sirens may be sounded. Listen to your radio or television for safety information.

General Emergency—Radiation could leak outside the plant and off the plant site. The sirens will sound. Tune to your local radio or television station for reports. Be prepared to follow instructions promptly.

Take Protective Measures

Before a Nuclear Power Plant Emergency

Obtain public emergency information materials from the power company that operates your local nuclear power plant or your local emergency services office. If you live within 10 miles, or about 16 km, of the power plant, you should receive these materials yearly from the power company or your state or local government.

During a Nuclear Power Plant Emergency

If a nuclear power plant emergency occurs, keep a battery-powered radio with you at all times, and listen to the radio for specific instructions. Close and lock doors and windows.

- **If Authorities Instruct You to Evacuate**—Leave immediately. *Do not* second-guess the instruction or seek out confirmation. Keep car windows and vents closed; use re-circulating air.
- **If Authorities Instruct You to Shelter in Place (or Stay Indoors)**—Close and lock all exterior doors and windows. Close vents, fireplace dampers, and as many interior doors as possible. Turn off air conditioners and ventilation systems to prevent drawing outside air into the building. Go to a basement, other underground area, or safe room, if possible. Seal the room by covering each window, door, and vent using plastic sheeting and duct tape. Fill all cracks and holes (including spaces around pipes and cracks under doorways). Do not use the telephone unless absolutely necessary.

If you suspect that you have been exposed to nuclear radiation, take these steps:

- Change clothes and shoes, taking care to keep the outside clothing surfaces from touching your bare skin.
- Put exposed clothing in a plastic bag.
- Seal the bag and place it out of the way.
- Take a thorough shower.

Keep food in covered containers or in the refrigerator. Food not previously covered should be washed before being put into containers.

After a Nuclear Power Plant Emergency

Seek medical treatment for any unusual symptoms, such as nausea, that may be related to radiation exposure. Follow the instructions for recovering from a disaster in Chapter 7.

CHAPTER 6

Terrorism

Throughout human history, there have been many threats to the security of nations. These threats have brought about large-scale losses of life, the destruction of property, widespread illness and injury, the displacement of large numbers of people, and devastating economic loss.

Recent technological advances and ongoing international political unrest are components of the increased risk to national security. Use this chapter to learn what actions to include in your family disaster plan to prepare for and respond to terrorist threats.

When you complete this chapter, you will be able to do the following:

- Recognize important terms.
- Take protective measures for terrorist threats.
- Know what actions to take if an event occurs.

GENERAL INFORMATION ABOUT TERRORISM

Terrorism is the use of force or violence against persons or property in violation of the criminal laws of most countries for purposes of intimidation, coercion, or ransom. Terrorists often use threats to accomplish the following:

- Create fear among the public.
- Try to convince citizens that their government is powerless to prevent terrorism.
- Get immediate publicity for their causes.

Acts of terrorism (in order of most common to least common incidents) include threats of terrorism; bomb scares and bombings; kidnappings and hostage taking; armed attacks and assassinations; arsons and firebombings; hijackings and skyjackings; cyber-attacks (computer-based); and the use of chemical, biological, nuclear, and radiological weapons.

High-risk targets for acts of terrorism include military and civilian government facilities, international airports, large cities, and high-profile landmarks. Terrorists might also target large public gatherings, water and food supplies, utilities, and corporate centers. Furthermore, terrorists are capable of spreading fear by sending explosives or chemical and biological agents through the mail.

Terrorism is a criminal act that influences an audience beyond the immediate victim. The strategy of terrorists is to commit acts of violence that draw the attention of the local populace, the government, and the world to their cause. Terrorists plan their attack to obtain the greatest publicity, choosing targets that symbolize what they oppose. The effectiveness of the terrorist act lies not in the act itself, but in the public's or government's reaction to the act.

The United States policy on terrorism is summarized as follows:

- All terrorist acts are criminal and intolerable, whatever their motivation, and should be condemned.
- The United States will support all lawful measures to prevent terrorism and bring those responsible to justice.
- No concessions will be made to terrorist extortion, because to do so only invites more terrorist action.
- When Americans are abducted overseas, the United States will look to the host government to exercise its responsibility to protect all persons within its territories, to include achieving the safe release of hostages.
- The United States will maintain close and continuous contact with the host government during the incident and will continue to develop international cooperation to combat terrorism.

Within the immediate area of a terrorist event, you would need to rely on police, fire, and other officials for instructions. However, you can prepare in much the same way you would prepare for other crisis events. General guidelines include the following:

- Be aware of your surroundings.
- Move or leave if you feel uncomfortable or if something does not seem right.
- Take precautions when traveling. Be aware of conspicuous or unusual behavior. Do not accept packages from strangers. Do not leave luggage unattended. You should promptly report unusual behavior, suspicious or unattended packages, and strange devices to the police or security personnel.
- Learn where emergency exits are located in buildings you frequent. Plan how to get out in the event of an emergency.

- Be prepared to do without services you normally depend on—electricity, telephone, natural gas, gasoline pumps, cash registers, ATMs, and Internet transactions.
- Work with building owners to ensure that safety items are located on each floor of the building, including the following:
  - Portable, battery-operated radio and extra batteries
  - Several flashlights and extra batteries
  - First-aid kit and manual
  - Hard hats and dust masks
  - Fluorescent tape to rope off dangerous areas

HOMELAND SECURITY ADVISORY SYSTEM

The Homeland Security Advisory System was designed to provide a national framework and comprehensive means to disseminate information regarding the risk of terrorist acts to the following:

- Federal, state, and local authorities
- The private sector
- The American people

This system provides warnings in the form of a set of graduated *threat conditions* that increase as the risk of the threat increases. Risk includes both the probability of an attack occurring and its potential gravity. Threat conditions may be assigned for the entire nation, or they may be set for a particular geographic area or industrial sector. At each threat condition, government entities and the private sector, including businesses and schools, would implement a corresponding set of *protective measures* to further reduce vulnerability or increase response capability during a period of heightened alert.

There are five threat conditions, each identified by a description and corresponding color. Assigned threat conditions will be reviewed at regular intervals to determine whether adjustments are warranted.

Threat Conditions and Associated Protective Measures

There is always a risk of a terrorist threat. Each threat condition assigns a level of alert appropriate to the increasing risk of terrorist attacks. Beneath each threat condition are some suggested protective measures that the government, the private sector, and the public can take.

In each case, as threat conditions escalate, protective measures are added to those already taken in lower threat conditions. The measures are cumulative.

Severe Risk of Terrorist Attacks — Red

- Complete recommended steps at levels orange, yellow, green, and blue.
- Listen to local emergency management officials.
- Stay tuned to TV or radio for current information/instructions.
- Be prepared to shelter or evacuate, as instructed.
- Expect traffic delays and restrictions.
- Provide volunteer services only as requested.
- Contact your school/business to determine status of workday.

High Risk of Terrorist Attacks — Orange

- Complete recommended steps at levels yellow, green, and blue.
- Exercise caution when traveling; pay attention to travel advisories.
- Review your family emergency plan, and make sure all family members know what to do.
- Be patient. Expect some delays, baggage searches, and restrictions at public buildings.
- Check on neighbors or others who might need assistance in an emergency.

Elevated Risk of Terrorist Attacks — Yellow

- Complete recommended steps at levels green and blue.
- Ensure disaster supplies are stocked and ready.
- Check telephone numbers in family emergency plan, and update as necessary.
- Develop alternate routes to/from work or school, and practice them.
- Continue to be alert for suspicious activity, and report it to authorities.

Guarded Risk of Terrorist Attacks — Blue

- Complete recommended steps at level green.
- Review stored disaster supplies, and replace items that are outdated.
- Be alert to suspicious activity, and report it to proper authorities.

Low Risk of Terrorist Attacks — Green

- Develop a family emergency plan. Share it with family and friends, and practice the plan.
- Create an "Emergency/Disaster Supply Kit" for your household.
- Know where to shelter and how to turn off utilities (power, gas, and water) to your home.
- Examine volunteer opportunities in your community, such as Citizen Corps, Volunteers in Police Service, Neighborhood Watch or others, and donate your time. Consider completing an American Red Cross First Aid or CPR course, or Community Emergency Response Team (CERT) course.

Summary

By following the instructions in this guide, you should now have:

- A family disaster plan that sets forth what you and your family need to do to prepare for and respond to all types of hazards
- A disaster supplies kit filled with items you would need to sustain you and your family for at least three days, maybe more
- Knowledge of your community warning systems and what you should do when these are activated
- An understanding of why evacuations are necessary and what you would need to do in the case of an evacuation
- Identification of where the safest shelters are for the various hazards

Compare the above actions with the personal action guidelines for each of the threat levels. Determine how well you are prepared for each of the five levels.

NOTE: To determine the current U.S. threat level, check your cable news networks or visit the U.S. Department of Homeland Security Web site at http://www.dhs.gov.

BOMB THREATS OR EXPLOSIONS

Terrorists have frequently used explosive devices as one of their most common weapons. Terrorists do not have to look far to find out how to make explosive devices; the information is readily available in books and through the Internet. The materials needed for an explosive device can be found in many places, including variety, hardware, and auto supply stores. Explosive devices are highly portable using vehicles and humans as a means of transport. They are easily detonated from remote locations or by suicide bombers.

Conventional bombs have been used to damage and destroy financial, political, social, and religious institutions. Attacks have occurred in public places and on city streets with thousands of people around the world injured and killed.

Packages that should make you suspicious include those that:

- Are unexpected or from someone unfamiliar to you.
- Have no return address or have one that cannot be verified as legitimate.
- Are marked with restrictive endorsements such as "Personal," "Confidential," or "Do not X-ray".
- Have protruding wires or aluminum foil, strange odors, or stains.
- Show a city or state in the postmark that does not match the return address.
- Are of unusual weight given their size, or are lopsided or oddly shaped.

- Are marked with threatening language.
- Have inappropriate or unusual labeling.
- Have excessive postage or packaging material, such as masking tape and string.
- Have misspellings of common words.
- Are addressed to someone no longer with your organization or are otherwise outdated.
- Have incorrect titles or titles without a name.
- Are not addressed to a specific person.
- Have handwritten or poorly typed addresses.

Take Protective Measures

If you receive a telephoned bomb threat, you should follow these guidelines:

- Get as much information from the caller as possible.
- Keep the caller on the line and record everything that is said.
- Use Caller ID or the *69 call-back feature, if available, to obtain the caller's telephone number
- Notify the police and the building management.

During an Explosion

If there is an explosion, you should do the following:

- Get under a sturdy table or desk if things are falling around you. When they stop falling, leave quickly, watching for obviously weakened floors and stairways. As you exit from the building, be especially watchful of falling debris.
- Leave the building as quickly as possible. *Do not* stop to retrieve personal possessions or make phone calls.
- *Do not* use elevators.

Once you are out:

- *Do not* stand in front of windows, glass doors, or other potentially hazardous areas.
- Move away from sidewalks or streets to be used by emergency officials or others still exiting the building.

If you are trapped in debris, do the following:

- If possible, use a flashlight to signal your location to rescuers.
- Avoid unnecessary movement so you do not kick up dust.
- Cover your nose and mouth with anything you have on hand. (Dense-weave cotton material can act as a good filter. Try to breathe through the material.)
- Tap on a pipe or wall so rescuers can hear where you are.

- If possible, use a whistle to signal rescuers.

- Shout only as a last resort. Shouting can cause a person to inhale dangerous amounts of dust.

After an Explosion

Call 9-1-1. Account for all of your family members and evacuate the area. Follow the instructions for recovering from a disaster in Chapter 7.

BIOLOGICAL THREATS

Historically, terrorist attacks using nuclear, biological, and chemical (NBC) weapons have been rare. Due to the extremely high number of casualties that NBC weapons can produce, NBC weapons are also referred to as weapons of mass destruction (WMD).

Biological agents are organisms or toxins that can kill or incapacitate people, livestock, and crops. The three basic groups of biological agents that would likely be used as weapons are bacteria, viruses, and toxins. Most biological agents are difficult to grow and maintain. Many break down quickly when exposed to sunlight and other environmental factors, while others, such as anthrax spores, are very long-lived. Biological agents can be dispersed by spraying them into the air, by infecting animals that carry the disease to humans, and by contaminating food and water. Delivery methods include the following:

- **Aerosols**—Biological agents are dispersed into the air, forming a fine mist that may drift for miles. Inhaling the agent may cause disease in people or animals.

- **Animals**—Some diseases are spread by insects and animals, such as fleas, mice, flies, mosquitoes, and livestock.

- **Food and Water Contamination**—Some pathogenic organisms and toxins may persist in food and water supplies. Most microbes can be killed, and toxins deactivated, by cooking food and boiling water. Most microbes are killed by boiling water for one minute, but some require longer. Follow official instructions.

- **Person-to-Person**—Spread of a few infectious agents is also possible. Humans have been the source of infection for smallpox, plague, and the Lassa viruses. Specific information on biological agents is available at the Centers for Disease Control and Prevention's Web site, http://www.bt.cdc.gov.

Take Protective Measures

Before a Biological Attack

To prepare for a biological threat, take these precautions:

- Check with your doctor to ensure all required or suggested immunizations are up to date. Children and older adults are particularly vulnerable to biological agents.

- Consider installing a High Efficiency Particulate Air (HEPA) filter in your furnace return duct. These filters remove particles in the 0.3 to 10 micron range and will filter out most biological agents that may enter your house. If you do not have a central heating or cooling system, consider using a stand-alone portable HEPA filter.

During a Biological Attack

In the event of a biological attack, public health officials may not immediately be able to provide information about what you should do. It will take time to determine what the illness is, how it should be treated, and who is in danger. Monitor television, listen to radio, or check the Internet for official news and information including signs and symptoms of the disease, areas in danger, if medications or vaccinations are being distributed, and where you should seek medical attention if you become ill.

The first evidence of an attack may be when you notice symptoms of the disease caused by exposure to an agent. Be suspicious of any symptoms you notice, but do not assume that any illness is a result of the attack. Use common sense and practice good hygiene.

If you become aware of an unusual and suspicious substance nearby, follow these guidelines:

- Move away quickly.
- Wash with soap and water.
- Contact authorities.
- Listen to the media for official instructions.
- Seek medical attention if you become sick.

If you are exposed to a biological agent, do the following:

- Remove and bag your clothes and personal items. Follow official instructions for disposal of contaminated items.
- Wash yourself with soap and water and put on clean clothes.
- Seek medical assistance. You may be advised to stay away from others or even quarantined.

Filtration in Buildings

Building owners and managers should determine the type and level of filtration in their structures and the level of protection it provides against biological agents; the National Institute of Occupational Safety and Health (NIOSH) provides technical guidance on this topic. Visit http://www.cdc.gov/NIOSH.

After a Biological Attack

In some situations, such as the case of the anthrax letters sent in 2001, people may be alerted to potential exposure. If this is the case, pay close attention to all official warnings and instructions on how to proceed. The delivery of medical services for a biological event may be handled differently to respond to increased demand. The basic public health procedures and medical protocols for handling exposure to biological agents are the same as for any infectious disease. It is important for you to pay attention to official instructions via radio, television, and emergency alert systems.

Using HEPA Filters

HEPA filters are useful in biological attacks. If you have a central heating and cooling system in your home with a HEPA filter, leave it on if it is running or turn the fan on if it is not running. Moving the air in the house through the filter will help remove the agents from the air. If you have a portable HEPA filter, take it with you to the internal room where you are seeking shelter and turn it on. HEPA filters will not filter chemical agents.

If you are in an apartment or office building that has a modern, central heating and cooling system, the system's filtration should provide a relatively safe level of protection from outside biological contaminants.

CHEMICAL THREATS

Historically, terrorist attacks using nuclear, biological, and chemical (NBC) weapons have been rare. Due to the extremely high number of casualties that NBC weapons can produce, NBC weapons are also referred to as weapons of mass destruction (WMD).

Chemical agents are poisonous vapors, aerosols, liquids, and solids that have toxic effects on people, animals, or plants. They can be released by bombs or sprayed from aircraft, boats, and vehicles. They can be used as a liquid to create a hazard to people and the environment. Some chemical agents may be odorless and tasteless. They can have an immediate effect (a few seconds to a few minutes) or a delayed effect (2 to 48 hours). While potentially lethal, chemical agents are difficult to deliver in lethal concentrations. Outdoors, the agents often dissipate rapidly. Chemical agents also are difficult to produce.

A chemical attack could come without warning. Signs of a chemical release include people having difficulty breathing; experiencing eye irritation; losing coordination; becoming nauseated; or having a burning sensation in the nose, throat, and lungs. Also, the presence of many dead insects or birds may indicate a chemical agent release.

Take Protective Measures

Before a Chemical Attack

To prepare for a chemical threat, take these precautions:

- Check your disaster supplies kit to make sure it includes the following:
  - A roll of duct tape and scissors.
  - Plastic for doors, windows, and vents for the room in which you will shelter in place. (To save critical time during an emergency, premeasure and cut the plastic sheeting for each opening.)
- Choose an internal room to shelter, preferably one without windows and on the highest level.

During a Chemical Attack

If you are instructed to remain in your home or office building during a chemical attack, you should do the following:

- Close doors and windows and turn off all ventilation, including furnaces, air conditioners, vents, and fans.
- Seek shelter in an internal room and take your disaster supplies kit.
- Seal the room with duct tape and plastic sheeting.
- Listen to your radio for instructions from authorities.

If you are caught in or near a contaminated area, you should do the following:

- Move away immediately in a direction upwind of the source.
- Find shelter as quickly as possible.

After a Chemical Attack

Decontamination is needed within minutes of exposure to minimize health consequences. Do not leave the safety of a shelter to go outdoors to help others until authorities announce it is safe to do so.

A person affected by a chemical agent requires immediate medical attention from a professional. If medical help is not immediately available, decontaminate yourself and assist in decontaminating others.

Decontamination guidelines are as follows:

- Use extreme caution when helping others who have been exposed to chemical agents.
- Remove all clothing and other items in contact with the body. Contaminated clothing normally removed over the head should be cut off to avoid contact with the

eyes, nose, and mouth. Put contaminated clothing and items into a plastic bag and seal it. Decontaminate hands using soap and water. Remove eyeglasses or contact lenses. Put glasses in a pan of household bleach to decontaminate them, and then rinse and dry.

- Flush eyes with water.
- Gently wash face and hair with soap and water before thoroughly rinsing with water.
- Decontaminate other body areas likely to have been contaminated; blot (do not swab or scrape) with a cloth soaked in soapy water, and rinse with clear water.
- Change into uncontaminated clothes. Clothing stored in drawers or closets is likely to be uncontaminated.
- Proceed to a medical facility for screening and professional treatment.

NUCLEAR THREATS

Historically, terrorist attacks using nuclear, biological, and chemical (NBC) weapons have been rare. Due to the extremely high number of casualties that NBC weapons can produce, NBC weapons are also referred to as weapons of mass destruction (WMD).

A nuclear blast is an explosion with intense light and heat, a damaging pressure wave, and widespread radioactive material that can contaminate the air, water, and ground surfaces for miles around. A nuclear device can range from a weapon carried by an intercontinental missile launched by a hostile nation or terrorist organization to a small portable nuclear device transported by an individual. All nuclear devices cause deadly effects when exploded, including blinding light, intense heat (thermal radiation), initial nuclear radiation, blast, fires started by the heat pulse, and secondary fires caused by the destruction.

Experts consider the danger of a massive strategic nuclear attack on the United States to be a very low risk. However, terrorism, by nature, is unpredictable.

If there were threat of an attack, people living near potential targets could be advised to evacuate, or they could decide on their own to evacuate to an area not considered a likely target. Protection from radioactive fallout would require taking shelter in an underground area or in the middle of a large building.

In general, potential targets include the following:

- Strategic missile sites and military bases
- Centers of government such as Washington, D.C., and state capitals
- Important transportation and communication centers
- Manufacturing, industrial, technology, and financial centers
- Petroleum refineries, electrical power plants, and chemical plants
- Major ports and airfields

The three factors for protecting oneself from radiation and fallout are distance, shielding, and time.

> **Distance**—The more distance between you and the fallout particles, the better. An underground area such as a home or office building basement offers more protection than the first floor of a building. A floor near the middle of a high-rise may be better, depending on what is nearby at that level on which significant fallout particles would collect. Flat roofs collect fallout particles so the top floor is not a good choice, nor is a floor adjacent to a neighboring flat roof.
>
> **Shielding**—The heavier and denser the materials—thick walls, concrete, bricks, books and earth—between you and the fallout particles, the better.
>
> **Time**—Fallout radiation loses its intensity fairly rapidly. In time, you will be able to leave the fallout shelter. Radioactive fallout poses the greatest threat to people during the first two weeks, by which time it has declined to about 1 percent of its initial radiation level.

Remember that any protection, however temporary, is better than none at all, and the more shielding, distance, and time you can take advantage of, the better.

Hazards of Nuclear Devices

The extent, nature, and arrival time of these hazards are difficult to predict. The geographical dispersion of hazard effects will be defined by the following:

- Size of the device—A more powerful bomb will produce more distant effects.
- Height above the ground the device was detonated—This will determine the extent of blast effects.
- Nature of the surface beneath the explosion—Some materials are more likely to become radioactive and airborne than others. Flat areas are more susceptible to blast effects.
- Existing meteorological conditions—Wind speed and direction will affect arrival time of fallout; precipitation may wash fallout from the atmosphere.

Radioactive Fallout

Even if individuals are not close enough to the nuclear blast to be affected by the direct impacts, they may be affected by radioactive fallout. Any nuclear blast results in some fallout. Blasts that occur near the earth's surface create much greater amounts of fallout than blasts that occur at higher altitudes. This is because the tremendous heat produced from a nuclear blast causes an updraft of air that forms the familiar mushroom cloud. When a blast occurs near the earth's surface, millions of vaporized dirt particles also are drawn into the cloud. As the heat diminishes, radioactive materials that have vaporized condense on the particles and fall back to Earth. The phenomenon is called radioactive fallout. This fallout material decays over a long period of time, and is the main source of residual nuclear radiation.

Fallout from a nuclear explosion may be carried by wind currents for hundreds of miles if the right conditions exist. Effects from even a small portable device exploded at ground level can be potentially deadly.

Nuclear radiation cannot be seen, smelled, or otherwise detected by normal senses. Radiation can only be detected by radiation monitoring devices. This makes radiological emergencies different from other types of emergencies, such as floods or hurricanes. Monitoring can project the fallout arrival times, which will be announced through official warning channels. However, any increase in surface buildup of gritty dust and dirt should be a warning for taking protective measures.

Electromagnetic Pulse

In addition to other effects, a nuclear weapon detonated in or above the earth's atmosphere can create an electromagnetic pulse (EMP), a high-density electrical field. An EMP acts like a stroke of lightning but is stronger, faster, and shorter. An EMP can seriously damage electronic devices connected to power sources or antennas. This includes communication systems, computers, electrical appliances, and automobile or aircraft ignition systems. The damage could range from a minor interruption to actual burnout of components. Most electronic equipment within 1,000 miles, or over 1,600 km, of a high-altitude nuclear detonation could be affected. Battery-powered radios with short antennas generally would not be affected. Although an EMP is unlikely to harm most people, it could harm those with pacemakers or other implanted electronic devices.

Take Protective Measures

Before a Nuclear Blast

To prepare for a nuclear blast, you should take these precautions:

- Find out from officials if any public buildings in your community have been designated as fallout shelters. If none have been designated, make your own list of potential shelters near your home, workplace, and school. These places would include basements or the windowless center area of middle floors in high-rise buildings, as well as subways and tunnels.
- If you live in an apartment building or high-rise, talk to the manager about the safest place in the building for sheltering and about providing for building occupants until it is safe to go out.
- During periods of increased threat increase your disaster supplies to be adequate for up to two weeks.

Taking shelter during a nuclear blast is absolutely necessary. There are two kinds of shelters:

- **Blast shelters** are specifically constructed to offer some protection against blast pressure, initial radiation, heat, and fire. But even a blast shelter cannot withstand a direct hit from a nuclear explosion.
- **Fallout shelters** do not need to be specially constructed for protecting against fallout. They can be any protected space, provided that the walls and roof are thick and dense enough to absorb the radiation given off by fallout particles.

During a Nuclear Blast

If an attack warning is issued, follow these guidelines:

- Take cover as quickly as you can, below ground if possible, and stay there until instructed to do otherwise.
- Listen for official information and follow instructions.

If you are caught outside and unable to get inside immediately:

- Do not look at the flash or fireball—it can blind you.
- Take cover behind anything that might offer protection.
- Lie flat on the ground and cover your head. If the explosion is some distance away, it could take 30 seconds or more for the blast wave to hit.
- Take shelter as soon as you can, even if you are many miles from ground zero where the attack occurred—radioactive fallout can be carried by the winds for hundreds of miles. Remember the three protective factors: distance, shielding, and time.

After a Nuclear Blast

Decay rates of the radioactive fallout are the same for any size nuclear device. However, the amount of fallout will vary based on the size of the device and its proximity to the ground. Therefore, it might be necessary for those in the areas with highest radiation levels to shelter for up to a month.

The heaviest fallout would be limited to the area at or downwind from the explosion, and 80 percent of the fallout would occur during the first 24 hours. People in most of the areas that would be affected could be allowed to come out of shelter within a few days and, if necessary, evacuate to unaffected areas.

Returning to Your Home

Remember to do the following:

- Monitor the radio and television for news about what to do, where to go, and places to avoid.

- Stay away from damaged areas. Stay away from areas marked "radiation hazard" or "HAZMAT." Remember that radiation cannot be seen, smelled, or otherwise detected by human senses.

Follow the instructions for recovering from a disaster in Chapter 7.

RADIOLOGICAL DISPERSION DEVICE (RDD) THREATS

Terrorist use of an RDD—often called *dirty nuke* or *dirty bomb*—is considered far more likely than use of a nuclear explosive device. An RDD combines a conventional explosive device—such as a bomb—with radioactive material. It is designed to scatter dangerous and sub-lethal amounts of radioactive material over a general area. Such RDDs appeal to terrorists because they require limited technical knowledge to build and deploy compared to a nuclear device. Also, the radioactive materials in RDDs are widely used in medicine, agriculture, industry, and research and are easier to obtain than weapons grade uranium or plutonium.

The primary purpose of terrorist use of an RDD is to cause psychological fear and economic disruption. Some devices could cause fatalities from exposure to radioactive materials. Depending on the speed at which the area of the RDD detonation was evacuated or how successful people were at sheltering in place, the number of deaths and injuries from an RDD might not be substantially greater than from a conventional bomb explosion.

The size of the affected area and the level of destruction caused by an RDD would depend on the sophistication and size of the conventional bomb, the type of radioactive material used, the quality and quantity of the radioactive material, and the local meteorological conditions—primarily wind and precipitation. The area affected could be placed off-limits to the public for several months during cleanup efforts.

Take Protective Measures

Before an RDD Event

There is no way of knowing how much warning time there will be before an attack by terrorists using an RDD, so being prepared in advance and knowing what to do and when is important. Take the same protective measures you would for fallout resulting from a nuclear blast.

During an RDD Event

While the explosive blast will be immediately obvious, the presence of radiation will not be known until trained personnel with specialized equipment are on the scene. Whether you are indoors or outdoors, at home or at work, you should be extra cautious. It would be safer to assume radiological contamination has occurred—particularly in an urban setting or near other likely terrorist targets—and take the proper precautions. As with any radiation, you want to avoid or limit exposure. This is particularly true of inhaling radioactive dust that results from the explosion. As you seek shelter from any location (indoors or outdoors) and there is visual dust or other contaminants in the air, breathe though the cloth of your shirt or coat to limit your exposure. If you manage to avoid breathing radioactive dust, your proximity to the radioactive particles may still result in some radiation exposure. If the explosion or radiological release occurs inside the building you are in, get out immediately and seek safe shelter elsewhere.

If You Are Outside When an RDD Event Occurs

- Seek shelter indoors immediately in the nearest undamaged building.
- If appropriate shelter is not available, move as rapidly as is safe upwind and away from the location of the explosive blast. Then, seek appropriate shelter as soon as possible.
- Listen for official instructions and follow directions.

If You Are Inside When an RDD Event Occurs

- If you have time, turn off ventilation and heating systems, close windows, vents, fireplace dampers, exhaust fans, and clothes dryer vents. Retrieve your disaster supplies kit and a battery powered radio and take them to your shelter room.
- Seek shelter immediately, preferably underground or in an interior room of a building, placing as much distance and dense shielding as possible between you and the outdoors where the radioactive material may be.
- Seal windows and external doors that do not fit snugly with duct tape to reduce infiltration of radioactive particles. Plastic sheeting will not provide shielding from radioactivity, nor from blast effects of a nearby explosion.
- Listen for official instructions and follow directions.

After an RDD Event

After finding safe shelter, those who may have been exposed to radioactive material should decontaminate themselves. To do this, remove and bag your clothing (and isolate the bag away from you and others), and shower thoroughly with soap and water. Seek medical attention after officials indicate it is safe to leave shelter.

Contamination from an RDD event could affect a wide area, depending on the amount of conventional explosives used, the quantity and type of radioactive material released, and meteorological conditions. Thus, radiation dissipation rates vary, but radiation from an RDD will likely take longer to dissipate due to a potentially larger localized concentration of radioactive material.

Follow these additional guidelines after an RDD event:

- Continue listening to your radio or watch the television for instructions from local officials, whether you have evacuated or sheltered in place.
- *Do not* return to or visit an RDD incident location for any reason.

Follow the instructions for recovering from a disaster in Chapter 7.

PERSONAL ANTITERRORISM MEASURES

As an American, you must be careful at home or when traveling abroad. Crime is a more common threat than terrorism; however, the threat of terrorism has a far greater impact on national security. You can narrow the chances of becoming a victim by increased awareness of potential problems and careful planning. Practicing sound individual protective measures makes you a so-called hard target.

Terrorists prefer a target that involves little risk and a high probability of success. Terrorists evaluate a target's security profile, predictability, and value. The target's value is determined by its importance and possible benefits gained. Once a target has been evaluated by terrorists, the target is labeled in the terrorist's mind as either a soft or a hard target.

Soft Targets

Soft targets are accessible, predictable, and unaware. They make it easy for strangers to access their private information (for example, phone numbers, addresses, schedules). Soft targets follow consistent routines at home and at work, allowing terrorists to predict a target's movements in advance. Soft targets are unaware of their surroundings and do not employ individual protective measures.

Hard Targets

Hard targets are inaccessible, unpredictable, and aware. They make it difficult for terrorists to gain access to themselves or their families. They vary their routes and vary their schedules. Hard targets consciously vary their routines and avoid setting patterns in their daily life. They are security conscious, aware of their surroundings, and proactively adhere to individual protective measures. Hard targets do not:

- Put their names on mailboxes or exterior walls of their homes.
- Run or walk daily at the same time of day or to the same place.
- Wash cars, mow lawns, or have family cookouts the same day every week.
- Shop the same day of each week at the same store.

- Travel to and from home on the same route and at the same time of day.
- Attend church services at the same time of day and place each week.
- Routinely sit in the same seat in a vehicle, restaurant, church, and so forth.
- Arrive at work, go to lunch, and depart work at the same time of day every day.
- Pick up the newspaper or mail at the same time of day every day.
- Walk or feed the dog along the same route or at the same time of day every day.
- Patronize the same restaurants or bars or patronize only American restaurants or bars.
- Park vehicles in the same area at church, social events, and so forth.

Identifying the Threat

Learn about your destination—the culture, language, local customs, and history of terrorist/criminal activity—as soon as you know that you're going to be traveling outside the United States. Information is available from these sources:

- The U.S. Embassy.
- The U.S. State Department consular information sheets, public service announcements or travel warnings via the Internet.
- Other Government agencies' manuals and Web sites.
- Newspapers, magazines, books, travel agents, or tourist offices.
- People who currently live or have lived in the area.

Once in-country, additional information is available from the U.S. Embassy and the host country; specifically:

- Are the terrorist groups in the area active?
- Are the terrorist groups organizing or reorganizing?
- What are the local populace's attitudes towards the terrorist groups?
- What are the local populace's attitudes towards Americans?
- Does the respective foreign government support, condone or condemn the terrorist activity?
- What is the potential for violence?
- What are the terrorists' methods of operation?

Generally, when a terrorist group is successful with a certain method of operation, the group reuses it or it will be used by other terrorist groups. However, just because a terrorist group has not used a specific tactic in the past does not mean they will not develop new tactics or adopt similar tactics used by other terrorist groups.

Limiting Visibility

Be alert to your surroundings, know and respect local customs and laws. Do not call undue attention to yourself. Be unpredictable by varying the days and times of your activities and by varying routes you usually travel.

Remember four basic rules:

- Be alert.
- Keep a low profile.
- Be unpredictable.
- Trust your instincts and common sense.

Anyone who is highly visible is a potential, high-risk victim. Victims can be targeted for being an American, a very important person (VIP), someone associated with VIPs, or a target of opportunity.

Avoid Identifying Yourself as an American

You can protect yourself from becoming a target if you avoid saying, doing, wearing, using, displaying or driving anything that readily identifies you as an American. Even if the local populace does not see Americans on a daily basis, global commerce and communications provides them access to magazines, movies, television shows, and Web sites that portray American lifestyles.

Clothing.   Blend in with what the local populace or local tourist element wears. Flashy or trendy clothing can attract unwanted attention. Clothes should not clearly identify you as an American (for example, cowboy boots, American logo T-shirts, clothes bearing American sports teams, and expensive athletic shoes).

Wear nonconspicuous civilian clothes when traveling back and forth to work. If you are working abroad and your job requires you to wear a uniform, change into your work dress after you arrive at work, and change into civilian clothes before you leave work.

License Plates.   Americans working overseas may be issued different colored license plates or a different number or letter indicator on their license plates. If possible, use local license plates on any automobile driven. Avoid using vanity license plates or license plates with conspicuous logos.

Speech.   The American dialect is hard to avoid, even if you speak the native language. Remember to avoid using American slang.

Customs and Habits.   Even if you physically blend in with the local populace, your customs and habits can identify you as an American. If possible, you should adopt local or tourist customs and habits.

Personal Behavior.   Some Americans have the tendency to be loud and obnoxious in the presence of the local populace. Another common mistake that Americans can make is to unnecessarily boast about American culture, wealth, technology, and military power, and so forth, in the presence of foreign nationals. Strive to blend in as much as possible, and not draw attention to yourself. *Keep a low profile*, especially in a public environment or with the local media.

Tattoos and Jewelry. Wear a shirt that covers tattoos with military, patriotic, or civilian slogans or logos when you go out. Leave military or patriotic jewelry—such as service rings, medallions, and watches—at home.

Controversial Materials. Familiarize yourself with local customs and practices before you travel. Avoid carrying potentially controversial materials such as gun magazines, American publications, religious books, pornography, or magazines that can offend the local populace.

Overt Patriotism. American flags, decals, patches, or logos easily identify you as an American. Avoid displaying them on your vehicles, clothes, and in front of your home or place of employment.

Currency. Exchange a few U.S. dollars into the local currency before arriving overseas. Use local currency and avoid carrying large amounts of money.

Avoid Identifying Yourself as a VIP

Many people, including terrorists, equate certain lifestyles with prominence. They believe that a prominent lifestyle is indicative of a person's importance to his government or company. Americans, in particular, are often treated by host governments as VIPs out of respect. Whenever possible, avoid being treated as a VIP.

Avoid using your title or position when introducing yourself or signing your name. Strive to maintain a low profile and blend in with the local populace. Avoid giving others the impression that you are important.

Expensive Cars. People may think anyone who drives an expensive car is important. Avoid driving expensive vehicles. Drive the type of vehicle that is common to the area in which you are located.

Bodyguards. If you do not need bodyguards, do not use them. If you must have bodyguards, keep them to a minimum and ensure that they blend in with the other personnel around you—they should not be obvious. Ensure bodyguards pass a background check and are well trained.

Chauffeurs. Many people may believe that anyone who has a driver is a VIP. Therefore, perform your own driving if possible. If you do have a driver, the rear right seat is typically reserved for a VIP. Therefore, sit up front with the driver and occasionally rotate your seat position within the vehicle. You should also do the following:

- Ensure your driver has the required training so that he will not panic or freeze in a high pressure situation.
- Develop an all-clear or distress signal (for example, a hat or cigarette pack on the dash) between you and your chauffeur. A signal allows the driver to warn you of a problem prior to your approaching the vehicle.
- Have the driver open the door for you.

- Avoid giving your itinerary to your driver. All a driver needs to know is when and where to be. For example, you have the driver show up at 7:00, but you do not leave until 8:00. If possible, tell your driver your destination only after the car has started.

Briefcases. In some countries, people think anyone carrying a briefcase is considered important. If possible, avoid carrying a briefcase unless it is the norm for the area. If the local populace uses backpacks, then you should also use a backpack.

Passports and Official Papers. Diplomatic (black) and official (red) passports indicate someone of importance. Use a tourist (blue or green) passport whenever possible. If you use a tourist passport, consider placing your official passport, military ID, travel orders, and related documents in your checked luggage. If you must carry official documents on your person, select a hiding place onboard your aircraft, bus, boat or train to hide them in case of a hijacking. Try to memorize your passport number and other essential information to avoid flashing this information in front of other passengers. While passing through customs, keep your passport out of sight by placing it in your airline ticket pouch.

Parking. VIPs warrant their own parking spots usually very close to their offices, thus drawing attention to themselves and their importance. Therefore, avoid using a designated parking space; instead, park in an unmarked parking space and rotate where you park your vehicle. Also, back your car into parking spaces so that you can exit quickly.

Domestic Employees. In many foreign countries domestic employees—such as maids, cooks, private guards, gardeners, and drivers—are very affordable. However, domestic help can provide terrorists with critical access to you and your family. If you are considering employing domestic help, ask for letters of reference and obtain a background check through the Embassy, if possible.

- Avoid live-in domestic help. If they must have access to keys, never let them remove keys from the house.
- Domestic employees should not allow anyone (including persons in police uniforms) to enter the house without permission from the family.
- Avoid providing transportation to and from work for any domestic employees. Pay for a taxi or bus fare.
- If a domestic employee calls in sick, do not accept the temporary services of a relative ("cousin" or "sister").
- Have domestic employees report potential terrorist surveillance of your residence and watch for anyone loitering in the area or repeatedly driving or walking by.
- Pay domestic help well and give cash rewards for following your security rules.
- Take special care to never discuss sensitive topics or detailed travel plans in their presence. Terrorists have successfully drawn this information from domestic employees in the past.

Avoid Identifying Yourself as a Target of Opportunity

When overseas, remember that you are a visual symbol of an American presence, values, prestige, and power. The longer you remain overseas, the more comfortable you may become. The more comfortable you become, the less you may think of yourself as a potential target. While overseas, never allow yourself to become complacent. Safeguard information concerning yourself, your home, job, income, and family. The more intelligence a terrorist can collect on you, the greater his chance of success. Terrorists gather their information from a variety of sources, including the following:

- Various Internet sources, including company Web pages.
- Bills of lading provide names of people moving into and out of an area.
- Immigration records provide names of people, dates of birth, and nationalities.
- Discarded mail or official correspondence can be used to identify an individual, the sender, and the place from which the correspondence was sent. Destroy any mail or official correspondence no longer needed, and remove address labels from magazines.
- The carbon from a credit card provides an individual's name and account number. Use the currency of the country you are visiting or working in. If you must use a credit card, also request the carbon copy.
- Checks can provide an individual's name, address, phone number, and social security number. Have only minimal information printed on the front of your checks.
- Nameplates make it easy to find an individual in an office environment; avoid their use, if possible.
- Do not keep business cards in your wallet, and do not hand them out casually.
- Receipts from hotels, laundries, and so forth, identify an individual by name and often by room number. Consider using a nickname or an assumed name.
- Luggage should be generic and civilian in nature. Avoid displaying your title or position, decals, or any American identifiers on your luggage.
- Remove all destination and baggage claim tags from luggage as well as stickers, decals, and other markings that reveal that the luggage has been through U.S. Customs (for example, custom's stickers).
- Be aware of all the documentation that contains information about your company, yourself, and your family. Destroy all documentation, especially trash, that could be used by terrorists as a source of information.

Family Members.   Family members must be aware of the potential terrorist and criminal threat at home and abroad. Ensure that your family members know and perform safeguards when traveling/living at home and abroad, including the following:

- The threat risk for the area.
- They must know where they are at all times. A simple orientation to the area could prevent them from straying into dangerous areas.

- Keep the house locked and secured whenever leaving the house. Exercise caution upon return. Set up simple signals to alert family members or associates if there is danger.
- Develop and practice emergency procedures for use in the home such as:
  - Evacuation due to fire
  - Intruders in the residence upon arriving home
  - Intruders breaking into the house
- Location and phone numbers of the U.S. Embassy, military base, neighbors, and all emergency services such as police, fire department, and medical services, and other safe locations for refuge or assistance.
- Memorize emergency phrases in the respective foreign language, and post these phrases by the telephone.
- In preparation for emergencies, maintain survival items (for example, supply of fresh water, nonperishable food, candles, lanterns, flashlights, extra batteries, blankets, portable radio, camping stove with spare fuel, axe, first-aid kit, and other appropriate items). Consider maintaining a similar kit for your car for emergency situations in isolated areas.
- Take an ample supply of medications that family members use. Also keep a copy of the prescription, statement from a physician, and know the generic name of the medication so you can reorder it abroad. Also, keep eyeglass prescriptions on hand.
- Always carry identification documents. Carry a card stating blood type and allergies to particular medications. The card should be bilingual/multilingual—English and the host nation language(s). Be prepared to dispose of these identifying articles should you be taken as a hostage.

Special Precautions for Children. Kidnapping is a potential tool used to extort ransom money that finances terrorist organizations or may be used as an attempt to force you to assist in a terrorist operation. Special precautions include the following:

- Never leave children alone or unattended. Leave children only with responsible and trustworthy individuals capable of handling emergency situations.
- Instruct children to keep doors and windows locked, and never to allow strangers into the house. Discourage children from answering the door, especially during hours of darkness.
- If possible, locate children's rooms in areas not easily accessible from the outside.
- Instruct children to never leave home without telling the parents. They should only travel in groups and avoid isolated areas especially when traveling to and from school. Accompany young children to and from bus stops, where necessary.
- Children should only use locally approved play areas where recreational activities are supervised by responsible adults and where police protection is readily available.

- Children should refuse automobile rides from strangers and refuse to accompany strangers anywhere on foot, even if a stranger says, "Your Mom/Dad sent me and said it was OK."
- Inform school authorities to never release children to any person who is not a family member. Instruct children to call home if a stranger is there to pick them up.
- Children should be told to refuse gifts from strangers and to avoid providing information to strangers such as their name and where they live.
- Children should immediately report anyone who attempts to approach them to the nearest person or authority (teacher, police).
- Instruct children not to discuss what you do and tell them to inform you if they are questioned about you by anyone.

Physical Security

Criminals remain the most likely threat in your home. However, terrorists have conducted operations at the homes of Americans overseas. Make your home a hard target. Develop a security plan that includes these components:

- **Outer Security**—Use available assets (local shop owners, neighbors, domestic employees, guards, family, etc.) to detect potential surveillance.
- **Inner Security**—Establish a warning system with pets, alarms, and motion sensors.
- **Barriers**—Fences, walls, locked doors and windows, secure rooms to go to in an emergency.
- **Communications**—Phone, cell phones, megaphones, intercoms, radios, audible alarms, linked security systems.
- **Deterrent/Response Systems**—Guards, pets, weapons (if authorized), and fire extinguishers.

General

- Change or rekey locks when you move in or when a key is lost by a family member. Maintain strict control of all keys. Change the security code in the garage door opener. Never leave house or trunk key with your ignition key while your car is being serviced or parked by an attendant.
- Do not open doors to strangers. Observe them through a peephole viewer. Establish procedures for accepting deliveries, such as verifying identities of delivery person, checking the identity of the deliverer with the appropriate dispatcher, and refusing all unexpected packages.
- Allow maintenance work only on a scheduled basis. Unless a clear emergency exists. Be alert to people disguised as public utility crews, road workers, vendors, and so forth, who might station themselves near the house to observe activities and gather information.
- Note parked or abandoned vehicles near the entrance or walls of the residence.
- Make residence appear occupied while you are away by using timers to control lights, TVs, and radios. Also do the following:

- Ask neighbors to pick up newspapers and mail.
- Schedule regular lawn work.
- Notify local law enforcement if you will be away for an extended period.

Residential Physical Security

- Routinely keep all doors, skylights, roof doors, and windows locked. Keep all window curtains and blinds tightly closed after sundown.
- Install lighting all around the house and yard; link to timers and sensors.
- Ensure door frames, doors, locks, and bolts are of solid construction. Ensure door hinges exposed to outside of house are pinned or spot-welded to prevent removal of the hinge bolt.
- Ensure fuse boxes are secure from tampering.
- Remove all trees, poles, ladders, and so forth, that might help an intruder scale fences, walls or gain access to second floor windows. Remove dense foliage or shrubbery near gates, garages, windows or doors that might conceal an intruder.
- Install intrusion detection, smoke, and fire alarms. Ensure intrusion detection alarms cover both the perimeter (doors and windows) and interior (motion and/or glass break sensors). Have the alarms monitored through a reputable security service or police. Train family members to use and test alarms regularly.
- If possible, select and prepare an interior safe room for use in case of emergencies. The safe room should have a sturdy door with a lock and an emergency exit, if possible. Bathrooms on upper floors are generally good, safe rooms.
- Store emergency and first-aid supplies in the safe room. Bars or grillwork on safe room windows should be locked from the inside to expedite escape.
- Keep keys to locks, a rope or chain ladder to ease escape, and a means of communication (for example, cellular phone and radio transmitter).

Telephones

- Do not place your name in a public local phone directory.
- If you receive obscene, threatening, or annoying phone calls or an unusual number of wrong or silent callers, report this to the police. Use caller-ID or call block, if available.
- Answer the phone without providing any personal information. Be especially cautious when sending personal information over computer online services.
- Report any interruption or unusual interference with phone, electrical, or computer service. This could be the first indication of "bugging" of your phone line.
- Keep a cellular phone charged and available, particularly at night.

Letter Bombs and Biological Mailings

Heightened personal security involves treating any suspicious looking mail (letter or package) as a bomb or a potential biological threat. If you think any mail is suspicious, contact the appropriate security officials, and let them investigate. Do not attempt to handle the mail yourself. You should examine your mail for the following suspicious features:

- Is it from a stranger or an unknown place?
- Is the return address missing?
- Is there an excessive amount of postage?
- Is the size excessive or unusual?
- Does it have external wires or strings that protrude?
- Is the spelling correct?
- Does the return address and place of postmark match?
- Does the handwriting appear to be foreign?
- Does it smell peculiar?
- Is it unusually heavy or light?
- Is it unbalanced (lopsided)?
- Are there any oily, sticky or powdery substances on the outside of the letter or package?
- Does it have springiness on the top, bottom or sides?

If you suspect that a piece of mail contains a bomb or biological agent, follow these guidelines:

- Do not panic.
- *Do not* shake the empty contents of any suspicious envelope or package. If any powder or substance leaks out, *do not* attempt to clean it up.
- Place the envelope or package in a plastic bag or some other type of container to prevent leakage of the contents. (If you do not have a container, cover the mail and do not remove the cover. If powder or any other substance has already leaked out, cover that also. You can cover the mail with clothing, paper, trash cans, etc.)
- Leave the room and close the door. Secure the area to prevent others from entering.
- Wash your hands with soap and water to prevent spreading any biological agent to your skin or respiratory system.
- Report the incident to authorities. If at home, dial 9-1-1 and report the incident to your local law enforcement agency. If at work, report the incident to the governing law enforcement agency and notify your building security official or an available supervisor.
- List all of the people who were in the room or area when the suspicious mail was recognized. Give this list to both the local health authorities and law enforcement officials.

Mail that is sent overseas should be delivered through the U.S. Embassy to allow for proper bomb detection and inspection by trained mail handlers.

Vehicle Bomb Search

A large number of terrorist attacks take place in or around a vehicle, typically by some sort of explosive device. This occurs because bombs are relatively easy to make and plant on exposed and unattended vehicles. Be familiar with your vehicle and the appearance of normal equipment under the hood so that you can search your vehicle for tampering and to recognize danger signs. By routinely inspecting your vehicle, you give the impression of being a hard target.

Travel

Traveling is one of the most opportune times for a terrorist attack. You are the most vulnerable and predictable in the morning as you enter or leave your residence, your place of work, or your vehicle. To reduce your chances of becoming a victim of a terrorist attack while traveling, follow the precautions listed below.

General Precautions

- Remain alert; travel in groups or pairs in well-lighted, busy areas.
- Watch your luggage at all times. Use concealed bag tags.
- Establish alternate routes from each starting place to each destination. Make sure at least one person you work with and someone in your family are aware of these routes and the approximate time it takes you to travel these routes.
- Keep travel arrangements confidential as much as possible.
- Avoid using your title or work addresses on tickets, travel documents, and hotel reservations.
- Make copies of important documents and place in different pieces of luggage: passport, ID card, and official papers. If lost or stolen, these items can be replaced at a U.S. Embassy, Consulate or military facility.
- Register with the U.S. Embassy upon arrival in country either in person or via phone. Carry a card that has the location and phone number of U.S. military facilities and the U.S. Embassy and Consulates in the area. These are vital safe havens during emergencies.
- Maintain a low profile. Do not discuss your personal or work matters with any other passengers.
- Avoid using public transportation. Buses and trains are preferred to a taxi. If you must travel in a taxi, specify the route you want the taxi driver to take and look for the photo identification or license to ensure that the photo matches the driver.
- Learn common phrases and greetings and how to ask for assistance or help in the local language.
- Know how to use public phones and carry enough change (in the local currency) to make a phone call. Calling cards can be used in many countries also.
- Learn the names and phone numbers of persons to contact at your destination, including emergency numbers.

Safeguards while Driving

- Park your car for easy escape (pointed outwards).

- Lock your car and garage when you park overnight. If possible, alternate use of parking garages. If you must park on the street, park in well-lighted areas.

- Walk to your car with keys in hand, ready to use.

- Perform a quick internal and external check of car.

- Start your car immediately after conducting your vehicle bomb search; do this before you adjust your seat or mirrors. You should be prepared for rapid escape if necessary.

- Lock your doors and keep your windows up.

- Wear your seat belt.

- Avoid traveling alone and during late hours. Know where the dangerous areas in the city are and avoid them.

- Travel only on busy, well-traveled thoroughfares, especially routes that allow speeds over 25 mph, or about 40 kph. Most attacks occur in stop and go traffic. Avoid one-way streets and other choke points such as bridges, traffic circles, and narrow alleyways. Avoid isolated secondary roads.

- Enter and exit your vehicle at busy locations.

- Know en route safe havens such as police and fire stations, military posts, and checkpoints you can drive to. If you feel you are being followed, do not go directly home.

- Vary times and routes driving to and from work.

- If possible, use different building entrances and exits.

- Keep your vehicle in good mechanical condition and your gas tank at least half full. Ensure you have a locking gas cap.

- Keep safety equipment (for example, cellular phone and fire extinguisher) inside your vehicle in good working order. Consider carrying a survival kit.

- Avoid driving close behind other vehicles or in any situation where you can get boxed in or forced to a curb. Have an evasive plan ready. Sometimes making a simple U-turn is enough to get you out of danger.

- Keep at least one-half car length of empty space in front of your vehicle when stopped at traffic signals and stop signs. This gives you room to escape in a kidnapping or armed attack/assassination attempt.

- Never pick up hitchhikers.

- In an emergency, drive on flat tires until reaching a well-lighted, well-traveled area or safe haven.

- In the event of mechanical failure, set out warning triangles/ flares, raise the hood, activate emergency flashers, and stay inside. If someone stops to offer assistance, ask them to notify the police or road service. If you feel unsure of the situation, do not get out of the car until the police or road service arrives. If you feel threatened by strangers, stay in the car with the doors locked. Use vehicle's horn to attract attention.

Safeguards while Walking

- Be alert to the possibility of surveillance. Before leaving a building or mode of transportation, check up and down the street for suspicious looking cars or individuals.
- Walk facing traffic at all times.
- Walk on the center of the sidewalk, this allows you to see around corners. Walking next to the street affords someone the opportunity to push you out into the street.
- Remain alert when walking across alley entrances or other places where a terrorist could be hiding.
- Walk only in lighted areas. Avoid bad sections of town.
- Avoid walking in noisy areas (for example, a construction site).
- Stay near people. Do not walk in isolated areas (for example, alleys).
- Avoid hostile crowds by turning back or crossing the street.
- If you suspect that you are being followed, move as quickly as possible to a safe haven (for example, police station or government office).

Safeguards while Flying

- If possible, buy your ticket at the last possible moment to prevent unauthorized personnel from finding out about your travel plans.
- Choose flights that will route you through an airport with a history of good security measures.
- Avoid countries, airports or airlines that are currently targets of terrorist organizations.
- Direct flights are best.
- Arrive early. Do not loiter near the ticket counter, luggage check-in or security area. Go through security as quickly as possible to the boarding area. Only use shops, restaurants, and lounges in the security area, not the main terminal.
- Buy your ticket at a travel agency that offers you seat selection and gives you a boarding pass when you buy your ticket. Ask for a window seat near the center of the aircraft. Terrorists generally select passengers for abuse that are sitting in more easily accessible aisle seats.
- Do not let your carry-on luggage out of your sight and do not agree to watch someone else's luggage.
- Keep your eyes open for any suspicious activity such as an individual who gets up and leaves behind bags, packages, and so forth. If you see something suspicious, get out of the area quickly and report it to airport security officials!
- Stay within the restricted or boarding areas of the airport, or leave the airport if possible or practical when you have a long layover for several hours.
- No matter where you are in the terminal, identify objects suitable for cover in the event of an attack. Pillars, trash cans, luggage, large planters, counters, and furniture can provide some protection.
- Sit with your back against a wall, facing the crowd to give you greater awareness to your surroundings.

- Avoid seats in first class.

- Count the number of seats to the closest emergency exit so that you will be able to find your way out in case the lights go out, or if the compartment fills with smoke.

- Even though flip-flops or slip-on shoes may make it quicker and easier to get through security, you should wear shoes that allow you to move unhindered in an emergency.

- Avoid telling other passengers that you are American or otherwise confiding in them. On a foreign carrier, avoid speaking English as much as possible.

- Inform someone of your destination and get in the habit of checking in with them before you depart and after you reach your destination. This could provide authorities with a starting point if you should become missing.

- At the first indication of a hijacking, hide all documents, identification cards, and official passports that could identify you as American.

Safeguards while Staying in Hotels

- Request another room if one has been reserved for you. Do not give your room number to strangers.

- Avoid street-level rooms. Ask for a room between the second and eighth floors. This puts you high enough to avoid easy access from the outside and still be low enough for local fire equipment to reach.

- Check before exiting from an elevator or your room for objects that seem out of place or for strangers who seem to be loitering.

- Answer the hotel phone with hello, not your name.

- Never answer hotel paging. If you are expecting someone, go to the lobby, but do not go to the desk and identify yourself, check to see if the caller is the person you are waiting for.

- Keep your room key on you at all times. Do not leave a copy of your room key on your key chain for the parking attendants.

- Be careful answering the door. First, check to see who it is through the peep hole or side window and arrange knock signals with your traveling companions.

- Watch for anyone loitering in halls, lobbies, or public areas or for anyone carrying objects that could be used as a weapon.

- Vary your arrival and departure times.

- Vary how you enter and exit the building; for example, use a hotel's entrance as well as its elevators and stairwells.

- Know where emergency exits and fire extinguishers are located.

- Avoid frequent exposure on windows and balconies. Keep your room draperies closed. Conduct business in your room, not in the lobby or hallways.

- Inspect your room thoroughly upon entering. Keep your room and personal effects neat and orderly. This practice helps you recognize tampering or strange, out-of-place objects.

- Place a piece of tape on the door crack or a string in the door jam. If it has moved while you were out, you will know that someone has entered your room during your absence.
- Lock the door and use the chain.
- Place the "Do Not Disturb" sign on the door.
- Avoid maid service and never admit a stranger to your room.
- Consider purchasing a portable door alarm, this will awaken you if someone attempts to enter while you are sleeping.
- Place a large screw into the space between the door and the door frame; this will delay anyone's entry into the room.
- Leave the lights, television or radio on when you are out of the room to give the appearance that someone is still there.
- Find out if the hotel has security guards; if so, determine how many, their hours of duty, equipment they use, their expertise, and how to locate them by phone and in person.
- Do not discuss travel plans over hotel phones. The lines could be "bugged."
- Do not take the first taxi in line when leaving your hotel and do not allow strangers to direct you to a specific cab.

Detecting Surveillance

Terrorist operations are normally meticulously planned, allowing for the greatest chance of success and safe escape for the terrorists. Reducing vulnerability with security enhancements is vital to your efforts to deter terrorist attacks. Equally important is surveillance detection. In most cases, the target that terrorists select to attack is based on lengthy surveillance. Through surveillance, they hope to learn about your habits and assess where you are vulnerable. By practicing good individual protective measures, you not only disrupt their intelligence gathering efforts, but you also make yourself a hard target. Terrorists want to hit soft targets, which minimizes their risk of failure. In cases of targets of opportunity, however, the surveillance may last only for a few minutes to hours to confirm the ease of the target. However, terrorists will usually abandon hard targets and move on to another soft target.

Upon arrival in a new area, begin determining what is normal and routine. Once you've determined what is normal and routine, it is easier to determine what is unusual. This makes the problem of identifying surveillance simpler. Often initial surveillance efforts are conducted by less experienced personnel who may often make mistakes. For example, terrorists will often show up at a surveillance location immediately prior to their target's arrival and depart immediately after the target leaves. A surveillance program involving family members, neighbors, and domestic employees can often detect this surveillance.

Look for people who are in the wrong place or dressed inappropriately. Eliminate stereotypes about terrorist surveillance personnel; they are often women and children. Be particularly observant when traveling to and from your home or office. Look up and down the streets for suspicious vehicles, motorcycles, mopeds, and so forth. Note people near your home or place of work who appear to be repair personnel, utility crews, or even peddlers. Ask yourself if they appear genuine or is something unusual?

Types of Surveillance

- **Stationary**—At home, along route or at work.
- **Following**—On foot or by vehicle.
- **Monitoring**—Telephone, mail, computers.
- **Searching**—Luggage, personal effects, trash.
- **Eavesdropping**—Electronic and personnel.

Terrorists sometimes employ an elaborate system involving several people and vehicles. Typical surveillance vehicles are motorcycles and cars with multiple personnel. Become familiar with local vehicle makes and models. Memorize and write down license plate numbers. Determine if a surveillance pattern is developing.

Surveillance Indicators

- Illegally parked or occupied parked vehicles.
- Cars with large mirrors.
- Cars that suddenly pull out of parking places or side streets when you pass, cars that move with you when you move, or cars that pass you and immediately park.
- Cars slowly maneuvering through turns and intersections or vehicles signaling for turns but do not turn.
- Flashing lights for signaling between cars.
- Unusual speeding up, slowing down or running red lights to stay up with you.

Conduct a route analysis of your principal routes that you make on routine trips. Identify choke points where your vehicle must slow down. Typically these choke points are traffic circles, one-way streets, bridges, and major intersections. Search out safe havens that you can pull into along the route in the event of emergency. If you think that you are being followed, go directly to a safe haven, not your home. Safe havens are generally well lit, public facilities where persons will respond to your request for help. (Examples of a safe haven might be a police station, fire station, large shopping mall, busy restaurant.)

If you are aware of surveillance, never let those watching you know you have figured out what they are doing. Never confront them. Terrorists and criminal elements are typically armed, do not want to be identified, and may react violently in a confrontation.

Reaction (if in a Vehicle)

- Circle the block for confirmation of surveillance.
- *Do not* stop or take other actions that could lead to confrontation.
- If possible, get a description of the car and its occupants.
- Go to the nearest safe haven. Report incident to the nearest security or law enforcement organization.

Reaction (if on Foot)

- Move rapidly towards a safe haven avoiding any route you routinely use.
- If a safe haven is not immediately available, move into a crowded area.
- Immediately report suspicions to nearest security element or local law enforcement.

Attack Recognition

If terrorists succeed in surveilling you and plan an attack, the next place to foil their efforts is to recognize their intentions and prepare to escape. Recognizing an attack scenario is difficult. Often what may appear to be an attack is more likely to be innocent circumstances. However, alertness and willingness to act are the keys to surviving a genuine attack scenario.

Abnormal Situations

- Individuals who appear to be excessively nervous and seem out of place by dress or mannerisms.
- Individuals wearing unusually long or heavy clothing for the environment.
- Individuals who appear to be acting as lookouts along your route of travel.
- Vehicles that hit your car from the front or rear.
- Unusual detours, vehicle roadblocks, cones, or other barriers. Be prepared to escape by going around the obstacle or ramming it.
- Vehicles traveling with items protruding from side doors or vans traveling with side doors open.
- Disabled vehicles, hitchhikers, or distressed "accident victims" seeking your assistance are commonly employed traps.
- A flagman, workman or fake police or government checkpoint stopping your car at a suspicious place.
- Sudden unusual activity or the unexplained absence of local civilians.
- Gunfire.

Escape, Evade, or Confront

Once you recognize an attack is occurring, decisions must be made immediately. If the scenario is an armed attack or assassination attempt, get out of the kill zone. Typically terrorists have a relatively narrow window of time and may have restricted fields of fire due to obstacles in their path. Once you exit the kill zone, terrorists will rarely pursue you since they must begin their own escape and evasion plan. In emergency situations, it may be a matter of survival to employ evasive driving techniques in order to arrive at the nearest safe haven. Use of evasive driving techniques may also be to you advantage by attracting the attention of local law enforcement. If on foot, take advantage of the density of crowds and layouts of buildings to evade pursuers. When you feel you have evaded the terrorists and are out of immediate danger, contact security forces or law enforcement for assistance.

In some cases, you may become captive as were the passengers on board the ill-fated flights of September 11, 2001. Escape and evasion were not possible. The only chance for those passengers to survive was to confront the terrorists in order to regain control of the aircraft. On one aircraft, although the plane crashed killing all on board, the passengers' confrontation with the terrorists saved countless lives because the aircraft never reached its intended target.

Incident Reaction

Bombs

Should a bomb explode outside the building, *do not* rush to the window to see what happened. Immediately seek cover in a protected area due to the possibility of a secondary, probably larger explosion (referred to as a double bombing). Terrorists may use an initial bomb to breach outer security, then a second bomb on the target, and may follow up the bombing with an armed attack. In a variation, terrorists can place an initial bomb, followed by a second bomb shortly thereafter to kill or injure security forces and emergency services responding to the initial bomb.

In the city, if you are on the street when a terrorist bomb explosion occurs, quickly get inside the nearest building and remain there. Shattered glass and other debris from high-rise buildings can fall for blocks around the point of explosion. As soon as practical following a bombing, take these steps:

- Notify the proper authorities.
- Evacuate the wounded based on the situation. Do not impede the efforts of emergency services. Witnesses to the bombing will naturally approach the explosion area to aid in searching for casualties. Authorities will also be trying to coordinate the search and will want to limit the number of searchers due to the threat of additional explosions and secondary effects such as falling masonry or fires.

- Move to a clear area, away from objects such as automobiles, buildings, and garbage containers.

Armed Attack or Assassination

If in an office or hotel, quickly lock the door, turn out the lights, grab the telephone, and get down on the floor. Call building security immediately. Telephone connections outside the building or hotel might be difficult to obtain. If no security office is available, call the local authorities. Tell the authorities exactly what you heard and provide them with the address, building, floor, room number, and telephone number. Stay in a protected area, and if possible, take the phone with you. If you believe you are involved in a terrorist takeover, hide your wallet and identification.

Arsons and Firebombings

Exercise normal fire safety precautions. However, do not gather in open areas such as parking lots or areas where others are congregating. Terrorists could stage an arson attack or false fire alarm to get a crowd out of a building and then conduct a bombing or armed attack.

CYBER-TERRORISM AND IDENTITY THEFT

Cyber-Terrorism

Cyber-terrorism is the leveraging of a target's computers and information technology, particularly via the Internet, to cause physical, real-world harm or severe disruption with the aim of advancing the attacker's own political or religious goals.

To protect yourself and your family, take these precautions:

- Use firewalls, antispyware, and antivirus software to protect your home computer.
- Use passwords containing a minimum of six characters that are difficult to guess containing both uppercase and lowercase letters, one or more numbers, and one or more special characters. Routinely change them.
- Routinely download software upgrades and patches from trusted sources.
- Do not open e-mail messages or access sites that seem suspicious or unsafe.
- Back up critical data on a regular schedule to an external hard drive or other media.
- Maintain hard copies (printed documents) of critical financial statements and other important data.
- Change your network configuration when you identify a threat or compromised security.
- Use secured wireless networks.

- Utilize log files to record protected action events.
- Monitor you family's Internet access and educate family members about the dangers of chat rooms and other social networking Web sites.

Identity Theft

Identity theft is wrongfully impersonating someone for financial or personal gain. A thief usually steals an identity by using knowledge of personal information about the subject.

To protect yourself and your family, take these precautions:

- Protect your personal information. Shred any documents containing personal or financial information before disposing of them in the trash. Collect delivered postal mail as soon as possible. Be wary of others when using an Automatic Teller Machine (ATM). Use firewalls, antispyware, and antivirus software to protect your home computer.
- Use gel ink pens when you write out checks (to prevent thieves from easily altering the information). Do not order checks preprinted with your driver's license and/or social security number.
- Never provide your credit card or other personal information to a company you do not know and trust.
- Know who you are dealing with.
- Always try to deal with brick and mortar companies. Avoid companies that do not readily and clearly state their name, physical address, and telephone number. You should be suspicious if they can only provide a Web address or a mail box drop.
- Do not rely on verbal promises. Get all promises in writing and review them carefully before you make any payments or sign any contracts.
- Read and understand the fine print in any written agreement.
- Do not pay up front for a loan or credit. Remember that legitimate lenders never "guarantee" a loan or a credit card before you apply, especially if you have bad credit, no credit, or a bankruptcy.
- Obtain and thoroughly review your credit report annually. The Fair Credit Reporting Act (FCRA) requires each of the nationwide consumer reporting companies (Equifax, Experian, and TransUnion) to provide you with a free copy of your credit report, at your request, once every 12 months. For more information, call (877) 322-8228.
- Stop preapproved credit card mail offers. FCRA requires each of the nationwide consumer reporting companies to provide consumers with the right to "Opt-Out" of lists provided to and used by creditors or insurers to make firm offers of credit or insurance that are not initiated by the consumer ("Firm Offers"). For more information, call (888) 567-8688.

CHAPTER 7

Recovering from Disaster

HEALTH AND SAFETY GUIDELINES

Recovering from a disaster is usually a gradual process. Safety is a primary issue, as are mental and physical well-being. If assistance is available, knowing how to access it makes the process faster and less stressful. This section offers some general advice on steps to take after disaster strikes in order to begin getting your home, your community, and your life back to normal.

Your first concern after a disaster is your family's health and safety. You need to consider possible safety issues and monitor family health and well-being.

Aiding the Injured

Check for injuries. Do not attempt to move seriously injured persons unless they are in immediate danger of death or further injury. If you must move an unconscious person, first stabilize the neck and back, then call for help immediately. Other guidelines for aiding the injured are as follows:

- If the victim is not breathing, carefully position the victim for artificial respiration, clear the airway, and commence mouth-to-mouth resuscitation.
- Maintain body temperature with blankets. Be sure the victim does not become overheated.
- Never try to feed liquids to an unconscious person.

Health

- Be aware of exhaustion. Don't try to do too much at once. Set priorities and pace yourself. Get enough rest.
- Drink plenty of clean water.
- Eat well.
- Wear sturdy work boots and gloves.
- Wash your hands thoroughly with soap and clean water often when working in debris.

Safety Issues

- Be aware of new safety issues created by the disaster. Watch for washed out roads, contaminated buildings, contaminated water, gas leaks, broken glass, damaged electrical wiring, and slippery floors.
- Carefully consider the safety risks before attempting extensive home repairs yourself. Many people become victims *after* a disaster because they attempt repairs (like roofing or electrical work) by themselves right after an event.
- Inform local authorities about health and safety issues, including chemical spills, downed power lines, washed out roads, smoldering insulation, and dead animals.

RETURNING HOME

Returning home can be both physically and mentally challenging. Above all, use caution.

General tips include the following:

- Keep a battery-powered radio with you so you can listen for emergency updates and news reports.
- Use a battery-powered flashlight to inspect a damaged home.

NOTE: The flashlight should be turned on outside before entering—the battery may produce a spark that could ignite leaking gas, if present.

- Watch out for animals, especially poisonous snakes. Use a stick to poke through debris.
- Use the phone only to report life-threatening emergencies.
- Stay off the streets. If you must go out, watch for fallen objects; downed electrical wires; and weakened walls, bridges, roads, and sidewalks.

Before You Enter Your Home

Walk carefully around the outside and check for loose power lines, gas leaks, and structural damage. If you have any doubts about safety, have your residence inspected by a qualified building inspector or structural engineer before entering.

Do not enter if any of the following apply:

- You smell gas.
- Floodwaters remain around the building.
- Your home was damaged by fire, and the authorities have not declared it safe.

Going Inside Your Home

When you go inside your home, there are certain things you should and should not do. Enter the home carefully and check for damage. Be aware of loose boards and slippery floors. Also, check for the following items:

- Natural gas—If you smell gas or hear a hissing or blowing sound, open a window and leave immediately. Turn off the main gas valve from the outside, if you can. Call the gas company from a neighbor's residence. If you shut off the gas supply at the main valve, you will need a professional to turn it back on. Do not smoke or use oil, gas lanterns, candles, or torches for lighting inside a damaged home until you are sure there is no leaking gas or other flammable materials present.
- Sparks, broken or frayed wires—Check the electrical system, unless you are wet, standing in water, or unsure of your safety. If possible, turn off the electricity at the main fuse box or circuit breaker. If the situation is unsafe, leave the building and call for help. Do not turn on the lights until you are sure they are safe to use. You may want to have an electrician inspect your wiring.
- Roof, foundation, and chimney cracks—If it looks like the building may collapse, leave immediately.
- Appliances—If appliances are wet, turn off the electricity at the main fuse box or circuit breaker. Then, unplug appliances and let them dry out. Have appliances checked by a professional before using them again. Also, have the electrical system checked by an electrician before turning the power back on.
- Water and sewage systems—If pipes are damaged, turn off the main water valve. Check with local authorities before using any water; the water could be contaminated. Pump out wells, and have the water tested by authorities before drinking. Do not flush toilets until you know that sewage lines are repaired/undamaged.
- Food and other supplies—Throw out all food and other supplies that you suspect may have become contaminated or come into contact with floodwater.
- Your basement—If your basement has flooded, pump it out gradually (about one-third of the water per day) to avoid damage. The walls may collapse, and the floor may buckle if the basement is pumped out while the surrounding ground is still waterlogged.
- Open cabinets—Be alert for objects that may fall.
- Clean up household chemical spills—Disinfect items that may have been contaminated by raw sewage, bacteria, or chemicals. Also clean salvageable items.
- Call your insurance agent—Take pictures of damages. Keep good records of repair and cleaning costs.

Being Wary of Wildlife and Other Animals

Disaster and life-threatening situations will exacerbate the unpredictable nature of wild animals. To protect yourself and your family, learn how to deal with wildlife.

Guidelines

- Do not approach or attempt to help an injured or stranded animal. Call your local animal control office or wildlife resource office.
- Do not corner wild animals or try to rescue them. Wild animals will likely feel threatened and may endanger themselves by dashing off into floodwaters, fire, and so forth.
- Do not approach wild animals that have taken refuge in your home. Wild animals such as snakes, opossums, and raccoons often seek refuge from floodwaters on upper levels of homes and have been known to remain after water recedes. If you encounter animals in this situation, open a window or provide another escape route, and the animal will likely leave on its own. Do not attempt to capture or handle the animal. Should the animal stay, call your local animal control office or wildlife resource office.
- Do not attempt to move a dead animal. Animal carcasses can present serious health risks. Contact your local emergency management office or health department for help and instructions.
- If bitten by an animal, seek immediate medical attention.

SEEKING DISASTER ASSISTANCE

Throughout the recovery period, it is important to monitor local radio or television reports and other media sources for information about where to get emergency housing, food, first aid, clothing, and financial assistance.

Direct Assistance

Direct assistance to individuals and families may come from any number of organizations, including the following:

- American Red Cross
- Salvation Army
- Other volunteer organization

These organizations provide food, shelter, supplies and assist in cleanup efforts.

The Federal Role

In the most severe disasters, the federal government is also called in to help individuals and families with temporary housing, counseling (for postdisaster trauma), low-interest loans and grants, and other assistance. The federal government also has programs that help small businesses and farmers. Most federal assistance becomes available when the president of the United States declares a so-called Major Disaster for the affected area at the request of a state governor. FEMA will provide information through the media and community outreach about federal assistance and how to apply.

COPING WITH DISASTER

The emotional toll that disaster brings can sometimes be even more devastating than the financial strains of damage and loss of home, business, or personal property. You should be especially aware of the immediate impact upon children and the elderly.

Understand Disaster Events

- Everyone who sees or experiences a disaster is affected by it in some way.
- It is normal to feel anxious about your own safety and that of your family and close friends.
- Profound sadness, grief, and anger are normal reactions to an abnormal event.
- Acknowledging your feelings helps you recover.
- Focusing on your strengths and abilities helps you heal.
- Accepting help from community programs and resources is healthy.
- Everyone has different needs and different ways of coping.
- It is common to want to strike back at people who have caused great pain.

Children and older adults are of special concern in the aftermath of disasters. Even individuals who experience a disaster secondhand through exposure to extensive media coverage can be affected.

Contact local faith-based organizations, voluntary agencies, or professional counselors for counseling. Additionally, FEMA and state and local governments of the affected area may provide crisis counseling assistance.

Recognize Signs of Disaster-Related Stress

Adults might need crisis counseling or stress management assistance when they display these signs:

- Difficulty communicating thoughts
- Difficulty sleeping
- Difficulty maintaining balance in their lives
- Low threshold of frustration
- Increased use of drugs/alcohol

- Limited attention span
- Poor work performance
- Headaches/stomach problems
- Tunnel vision/muffled hearing
- Colds or flulike symptoms
- Disorientation or confusion
- Difficulty concentrating
- Reluctance to leave home
- Depression, sadness
- Feelings of hopelessness
- Mood swings and easy bouts of crying
- Overwhelming guilt and self-doubt
- Fear of crowds, strangers, or being alone

Easing Disaster-Related Stress

Ways to ease disaster-related stress include the following:

- Talk with someone about your feelings—anger, sorrow, and other emotions—even though it may be difficult.
- Seek help from professional counselors who deal with postdisaster stress.
- Do not hold yourself responsible for the disastrous event or be frustrated because you feel you cannot help directly in the rescue work.
- Take steps to promote your own physical and emotional healing by healthy eating, rest, exercise, relaxation, and meditation.
- Maintain a normal family and daily routine, limiting demanding responsibilities on yourself and your family.
- Spend time with family and friends.
- Participate in memorials.
- Use existing support groups of family, friends, and religious institutions.
- Ensure you are ready for future events by restocking your disaster supplies kits and updating your family disaster plan. Doing these positive actions can be comforting.

Helping Children Cope with Disaster

Disasters can leave children feeling frightened, confused, and insecure. Whether a child has personally experienced trauma, has merely seen the event on television, or has heard it discussed by adults, it is important for parents and teachers to be informed and ready to help if reactions to stress begin to occur.

Children may respond to disaster by demonstrating fears, sadness, or behavioral problems. Younger children may return to earlier behavior patterns, such as bed-wetting, sleep problems, and separation anxiety. Older children may also display anger, aggression, school problems, or withdrawal. Some children who have only indirect contact with the disaster but witness it on television may develop distress.

Who Is at Risk?

For many children, reactions to disasters are brief and represent normal reactions to abnormal events. A smaller number of children can be at risk for more enduring psychological distress as a function of three major risk factors:

- Direct exposure to the disaster, such as being evacuated, observing injuries or death of others, or experiencing injury along with fearing one's life is in danger.
- Loss/grief—This relates to the death or serious injury of family or friends.
- Ongoing stress from the secondary effects of disaster, such as temporarily living elsewhere, loss of friends and social networks, loss of personal property, parental unemployment, and costs incurred during recovery to return the family to predisaster life and living conditions.

What Creates Vulnerabilities in Children?

In most cases, depending on the risk factors above, distressing responses are temporary. In the absence of severe threat to life, injury, loss of loved ones, or secondary problems such as loss of home, moves, and so forth, symptoms usually diminish over time. For those who were directly exposed to the disaster, reminders of the disaster, such as high winds, smoke, cloudy skies, sirens, or other reminders, may cause upsetting feelings to return. Having a prior history of some type of traumatic event or severe stress may contribute to these feelings.

Children often cope with disasters or emergencies the way parents cope. They can detect adults' fears and sadness. Parents and adults can make disasters less traumatic for children by taking steps to manage their own feelings and plans for coping. Parents are almost always the best source of support for children in disasters. One way to establish a sense of control and to build confidence in children before a disaster is to engage and involve them in preparing a family disaster plan. After a disaster, children can contribute to a family recovery plan.

A Child's Reaction to Disaster by Age

Listed below are common reactions in children after a disaster or traumatic event:

Birth through 2 years—When children are preverbal and experience a trauma, they do not have the words to describe the event or their feelings. However, they can retain memories of particular sights, sounds, or smells. Infants may react to trauma by being irritable, crying more than usual, or wanting to be held and cuddled. The biggest influence on children of this age is how their parents cope. As children get older, their play may involve acting out elements of the traumatic event that occurred several years in the past and was seemingly forgotten.

Preschool, 3 through 6 years—Preschool children often feel helpless and powerless in the face of an overwhelming event. Because of their age and small size, they lack the ability to protect themselves or others. As a result, they feel intense fear and insecurity about being separated from caregivers. Preschoolers cannot grasp the concept of permanent loss. They can see consequences as being reversible or permanent. In the weeks following a traumatic event, preschoolers' play activities may reenact the incident or the disaster over and over again.

School age, 7 through 10 years—The school-age child has the ability to understand the permanence of loss. Some children become intensely preoccupied with the details of a traumatic event and want to talk about it continually. This preoccupation can interfere with the child's concentration at school, and academic performance may decline. At school, children may hear inaccurate information from peers. They may display a wide range of reactions—sadness, generalized fear, or specific fears of the disaster happening again; guilt over action or inaction during the disaster; anger that the event was not prevented; or fantasies of playing rescuer.

Preadolescence to adolescence, 11 through 18 years—As children grow older, they develop a more sophisticated understanding of the disaster event. Their responses are more similar to adults. Teenagers may become involved in dangerous risk-taking behaviors, such as reckless driving or alcohol or drug use. Others can become fearful of leaving home and avoid previous levels of activities. Much of adolescence is focused on moving out into the world. After a trauma, the view of the world can seem more dangerous and unsafe. A teenager may feel overwhelmed by intense emotions and yet feel unable to discuss them with others.

Meeting the Child's Emotional Needs

Children's reactions are influenced by the behavior, thoughts, and feelings of adults. Adults should encourage children and adolescents to share their thoughts and feelings about the incident. Clarify misunderstandings about risk and danger by listening to children's concerns and answering questions. Maintain a sense of calm by validating children's concerns and perceptions and with discussion of concrete plans for safety.

Listen to what the child is saying. If a young child is asking questions about the event, answer them simply without the elaboration needed for an older child or adult. Some children are comforted by knowing more or less information than others; decide what level of information your particular child needs. If a child has difficulty expressing feelings, allow the child to draw a picture or tell a story about what happened.

Try to understand what is causing anxieties and fears. Be aware that following a disaster, children are most afraid of the following:

- The event will happen again.
- Someone close to them will be killed or injured.
- They will be left alone or separated from the family.

Reassuring Children After a Disaster

Suggestions to help reassure children include the following:

- Personal contact is reassuring. Hug and touch your children.
- Calmly provide factual information about the recent disaster and current plans for insuring their safety along with recovery plans.
- Encourage your children to talk about their feelings.
- Spend extra time with your children, such as at bedtime.
- Reestablish your daily routine for work, school, play, meals, and rest.
- Involve your children by giving them specific chores to help them feel they are helping to restore family and community life.
- Praise and recognize responsible behavior.
- Understand that your children will have a range of reactions to disasters.
- Encourage your children to help update your family disaster plan.

If you have tried to create a reassuring environment by following the steps above and your child continues to exhibit stress; if the reactions worsen over time; or if your child's reactions cause interference with daily behavior at school, at home, or with other relationships, it may be appropriate to talk to a professional. You can get professional help from the child's primary care physician, a mental health provider specializing in children's needs, or a member of the clergy.

Monitor and Limit Your Family's Exposure to the Media

News coverage related to a disaster may elicit fear and confusion and arouse anxiety in children. This is particularly true for large-scale disasters or a terrorist event where significant property damage and loss of life has occurred. Particularly for younger children, repeated images of an event may cause them to believe the event is recurring over and over.

If parents allow children to watch television or use the Internet where images or news about the disaster are shown, parents should be with them to encourage communication and provide explanations. This may also include parents' monitoring and appropriately limiting their own exposure to anxiety-provoking information.

Use Support Networks

Parents help their children when they take steps to understand and manage their own feelings and ways of coping. They can do this by building and using social support systems of family, friends, community organizations and agencies, faith-based institutions, or other resources that work for that family. Parents can build their own unique social support systems so that in an emergency situation or when a disaster strikes, they can be supported and helped to manage their reactions. As a result, parents will be more available to their children and better able to support them. Parents are almost always the best source of support for children in difficult times. But to support their children, parents need to attend to their own needs and have a plan for their own support.

Preparing for disaster helps everyone in the family accept the fact that disasters do happen and provides an opportunity to identify and collect the resources needed to meet basic needs after disaster. Preparation helps—when people feel prepared, they cope better, and so do children.

HELPING OTHERS

The compassion and generosity of the American people is never more evident than after a disaster. People want to help. Here are some general guidelines on helping others after a disaster:

- Volunteer! Check with local organizations, or listen to local news reports for information about where volunteers are needed.

   NOTE: Until volunteers are specifically requested, stay away from disaster areas.

- Bring your own food, water, and emergency supplies to a disaster area if you are needed there. This is especially important in cases where a large area has been affected and emergency items are in short supply.
- Give a check or money order to a recognized disaster relief organization. These groups are organized to process checks, purchase what is needed, and get it to the people who need it most.
- Do not drop off food, clothing, or any other item to a government agency or disaster relief organization unless a particular item has been requested. Normally, these organizations do not have the resources to sort through the donated items.
- Donate a quantity of a given item or class of items (such as nonperishable food) rather than a mix of different items. Determine where your donation is going, how it's going to get there, who is going to unload it, and how it is going to be distributed. Without sufficient planning, much-needed supplies will be left unused.

Appendix A

Water Conservation Tips

INDOOR WATER CONSERVATION TIPS

General

- Never pour water down the drain when there may be another use for it. Use it to water your indoor plants or garden.
- Repair dripping faucets by replacing washers. One drop per second wastes 2,700 gallons, or about 10,220 liters, of water per year!
- Check all plumbing for leaks. Have leaks repaired by a plumber.
- Retrofit all household faucets by installing aerators with flow restrictors.
- Install an instant hot water heater on your sink.
- Insulate your water pipes to reduce heat loss and prevent them from breaking.
- Install a water-softening system only when the minerals in the water would damage your pipes. Turn the softener off while on vacation.
- Choose appliances that are more energy and water efficient.

Bathroom

- Consider purchasing a low-volume toilet that uses less than half the water of older models.

    NOTE: In many areas, low-volume units are required by law.

- Install a toilet displacement device to cut down on the amount of water needed to flush the toilet. Place a one-gallon (four-liter) plastic jug of water into the tank to displace toilet flow (do not use a brick, it may dissolve and loose pieces may cause damage to the internal parts). Be sure installation does not interfere with the operating parts.

- Replace your showerhead with an ultra-low-flow version.
- Place a bucket in the shower to catch excess water for watering plants.
- Avoid flushing the toilet unnecessarily. Dispose of tissues and other similar waste in the trash rather than the toilet.
- Avoid taking baths. Instead, take short showers—turn on water only to get wet and lather and then again to rinse off.
- Avoid letting the water run while brushing your teeth, washing your face, or shaving.

Kitchen

- Operate automatic dishwashers only when they are fully loaded. Use the light-wash feature, if available, to use less water.
- Hand wash dishes by filling two containers—one with soapy water and the other with rinse water containing a small amount of chlorine bleach.
- Clean vegetables in a pan filled with water rather than running water from the tap.
- Start a compost pile as an alternate method of disposing of food waste, or simply dispose of food in the garbage. (Kitchen sink disposals require a lot of water to operate properly.)
- Store drinking water in the refrigerator. Do not let the tap run while you are waiting for water to cool.
- Avoid wasting water while waiting for it to get hot. Capture it for other uses such as plant watering, or heat it on the stove or in a microwave.
- Avoid rinsing dishes before placing them in the dishwasher; just remove large particles of food. (Most dishwashers can clean soiled dishes very well, so dishes do not have to be rinsed before washing.)
- Avoid using running water to thaw meat or other frozen foods. Defrost food overnight in the refrigerator, or use the defrost setting on your microwave oven.

Laundry

- Operate automatic clothes washers only when they are fully loaded, or set the water level for the size of your load.

OUTDOOR WATER CONSERVATION TIPS

General

- Check your well pump periodically. If the automatic pump turns on and off while water is not being used, you have a leak.
- Plant native or drought-tolerant grasses, ground covers, shrubs, and trees. Once established, they do not need water as frequently and usually will survive a dry

period without watering. Small plants require less water to become established. Place plants together based on similar water needs.

- Install irrigation devices that are the most water efficient for each use. Micro- and drip-irrigation and soaker hoses are examples of efficient devices.
- Use mulch to retain moisture in the soil. Mulch also helps control weeds that compete with landscape plants for water.
- Avoid purchasing recreational water toys that require a constant stream of water.
- Avoid installing ornamental water features (such as fountains) unless they use recycled water.

Car Washing

- Use a shutoff nozzle that can be adjusted down to a fine spray on your hose.
- Use a commercial car wash that recycles water. If you wash your own car, park on the grass so that you will be watering it at the same time.

Lawn Care

- Avoid overwatering your lawn. A heavy rain eliminates the need for watering for up to two weeks. Most of the year, lawns only need one inch, or about 2.5 centimeters, of water per week.
- Water in several short sessions rather than one long one, in order for your lawn to better absorb moisture.
- Position sprinklers so that water lands on the lawn and shrubs, and not on paved areas.
- Avoid sprinklers that spray a fine mist. Mist can evaporate before it reaches the lawn. Check sprinkler systems and timing devices regularly to be sure they operate properly.
- Raise the lawn mower blade to at least three inches, or about 8 centimeters, or to its highest level. A higher cut encourages grass roots to grow deeper, shades the root system, and holds soil moisture.
- Plant drought-resistant lawn seed.
- Avoid overfertilizing your lawn. Applying fertilizer increases the need for water. Apply fertilizers that contain slow-release, water-insoluble forms of nitrogen.
- Use a broom or blower instead of a hose to clean leaves and other debris from your driveway or sidewalk.
- Avoid leaving sprinklers or hoses unattended. A garden hose can pour out 600 gallons, or about 2,270 liters, or more in only a few hours.

Pool

- Install a new water-saving pool filter. A single back flushing with a traditional filter uses 180 to 250 gallons, or over 900 liters, of water.
- Cover pools and spas to reduce evaporation of water.

APPENDIX B

Disaster Supplies Checklists

Keep lists to help you determine what to include in your disaster supplies kit. Consider those items that will meet your family's needs.

FIRST-AID SUPPLIES

In your home, make sure that you keep these items in a watertight container, protected from animals. For example, you might consider using a large plastic garbage can with a latching lid.

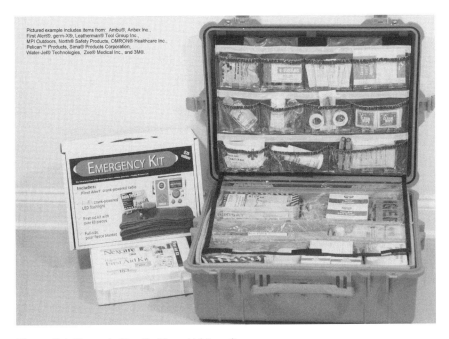

Figure B.1: Example Family First-Aid Supplies

Table B.1
First-Aid Supplies

First-aid items	Unit	Home	Car	Office
Basic first-aid manual	1 each	☐	☐	☐
Copy of this checklist/inventory	1 each	☐	☐	☐
Adhesive bandages, various sizes	1 box	☐	☐	☐
5" × 9" sterile dressing	1 each	☐	☐	☐
Conforming roller gauze bandage	1 each	☐	☐	☐
Triangular bandages	3 each	☐	☐	☐
3" × 3" sterile gauze pads	2 each	☐	☐	☐
4" × 4" sterile gauze pads	2 each	☐	☐	☐
3" cohesive bandage	1 roll	☐	☐	☐
Bandages for burns (Second Skin) 3" × 3 1/2"	2 each	☐	☐	☐
Butterfly sutures or Leukostrips	1 box	☐	☐	☐
Waterless, alcohol-based hand sanitizer	1 bottle, large	☐	☐	☐
Antiseptic wipes	1 box	☐	☐	☐
Large, medical grade, nonlatex gloves	6 pairs	☐	☐	☐
NIOSH-approved N95 air-purifying respirator	1 each	☐	☐	☐
Tongue-depressor blades	1 box	☐	☐	☐
Adhesive tape, 2" width	2 rolls	☐	☐	☐
Antibacterial ointment	1 tube	☐	☐	☐
Cold pack (reusable)	1 each	☐	☐	☐
Eyedropper	1 each	☐	☐	☐
Scissors (small, personal)	1 each	☐	☐	☐
Tweezers	1 each	☐	☐	☐
Scalpel	1 each	☐	☐	☐
Safety pins, assorted sizes	1 box	☐	☐	☐
Cotton balls	1 bag	☐	☐	☐
Cotton swabs	1 box	☐	☐	☐
Thermometer (not mercury, preferably digital)	1 each	☐	☐	☐
Isopropyl alcohol	1 bottle	☐	☐	☐
Petroleum jelly	1 tube	☐	☐	☐
Sunscreen	1 each	☐	☐	☐
Insect repellent	1 each	☐	☐	☐
SAM® splint	1 each	☐	☐	☐
Snakebite kit	1 each	☐	☐	☐
CPR breathing barrier, such as a face shield	1 each	☐	☐	☐

NONPRESCRIPTION AND PRESCRIPTION MEDICINE KIT SUPPLIES

Store these supplies in a watertight container (for example, a large plastic garbage can with a latching lid) along with your family first-aid kit, hygiene items, nonperishable food, and emergency water. Keep this container protected from animals in a logical place on the main floor of your home.

Table B.2
Medicine Kit Supplies

Medicine-kit items	Unit	Home	Car	Office
Aspirin and nonaspirin pain reliever	1 bottle	☐	☐	☐
Ibuprofen	1 bottle	☐	☐	☐
Analgesic cream	1 tube	☐	☐	☐
Antidiarrhea medication	1 each	☐	☐	☐
Antifungal medication	1 each	☐	☐	☐
Antacid (for stomach upset)	1 each	☐	☐	☐
Antibiotic (may require a doctor's prescription)	1 series	☐	☐	☐
Antihistamine	1 box	☐	☐	☐
Antiseptic ointment	1 tube	☐	☐	☐
Burn ointment	1 tube	☐	☐	☐
Bicarbonate of soda	1 box	☐	☐	☐
Epsom salts	1 box	☐	☐	☐
Laxative	1 each	☐	☐	☐
Eyedrops	1 bottle	☐	☐	☐
Itching/rash treatment	1 bottle	☐	☐	☐
Vomit inducer (Ipecac)	1 bottle	☐	☐	☐
Poison absorber (activated charcoal)	1 each	☐	☐	☐
Lip balm	1 tube	☐	☐	☐
Sunburn relief	1 each	☐	☐	☐
Multivitamins	1 each	☐	☐	☐
Prescriptions (at least 30-day supply)	1 each	☐	☐	☐
Extra eyeglasses/contact lenses	1 each	☐	☐	☐
Antitoxin (DMSO)	1 each	☐	☐	☐
Radiation protection (KI or KIO3)	1 each	☐	☐	☐

SANITATION AND HYGIENE SUPPLIES

Make sure you keep these items in a watertight container (for example, a large plastic garbage can with a latching lid), protected from animals.

Table B.3
Hygiene Supplies

Hygiene supplies	Unit	Home kit
Washcloth and towel	2 each	☐
Towelettes, soap, hand sanitizer	2 each	☐
Toothpaste, toothbrushes, dental floss	1 each	☐
Shampoo, comb, and brush	1 each	☐
Deodorants, sunscreen	1 each	☐
Razor, shaving cream	1 each	☐
Lip balm	1 each	☐
Insect repellent	1 each	☐
Contact lens solutions	1 each	☐
Mirror	1 each	☐
Feminine supplies	1 box	☐
Toilet paper	2 rolls	☐
5-gallon bucket with tight-sealing lid	1 each	☐
Small shovel for digging a latrine	1 each	☐
Disinfectant and household chlorine bleach	1 bottle	☐
Heavy-duty plastic garbage bags and ties	1 box	☐

TOOLS AND EQUIPMENT

In an emergency, you do not want to concern yourself with searching for a flashlight or other critical tools. Store these things with your other emergency supplies in a logical place (for example, a pantry or a closet on the main floor of your home).

Figure B.2: Example Family Emergency Gear Kit

Table B.4
Emergency Tools and Equipment

General tools	Unit	Home kit
NOAA Weather Radio (hand-crank charger)	1 each	☐
Flashlight and extra batteries	3 each	☐
Cellular telephone	1 each	☐
Multi-Tool or all-purpose knife	1 each	☐
Signal flare	3 each	☐
Chemical light sticks	12 each	☐
Matches in a waterproof container	1 each	☐
Utility Shutoff wrench, shovel, and handsaw	1 each	☐
Duct tape and scissors	1 each	☐
Plastic sheeting	1 roll	☐
Whistle	1 each	☐
Signal mirror	1 each	☐
Small canister, ABC-type fire extinguisher	1 each	☐
Emergency escape ladder	1 each	☐
Tube tent or shelter half	1 each	☐
Emergency blanket	1 each	☐
Compass	1 each	☐
Work gloves	1 pair	☐
Paper, pens, and pencils	1 each	☐
Needles and thread	1 kit	☐
Windup clock	1 each	☐
Kitchen tools		
Manual can opener	1 each	☐
Paper/plastic cups, plates, and plastic utensils	1 pack each	☐
Household liquid bleach to treat drinking water	1 bottle	☐
Sugar, salt, pepper	1 each	☐
Aluminum foil and plastic wrap	1 box each	☐
Resealing plastic bags	1 box	☐
Small cooking stove and a can of cooking fuel	1 each	☐

FOOD AND WATER

Store food and water with your family emergency supplies and rotate these items regularly. Also, make sure that each family member knows where these supplies are kept and what is stored in the watertight container(s).

Table B.5
Emergency Food and Water

Supplies	Unit	Home	Car	Office
Water (3-day supply; 1 gallon/person/day)	3 days' worth	☐	☐	☐
Ready-to-eat meats, fruits, and vegetables	3 days' worth	☐	☐	☐
Canned or boxed juices, milk, and soup	3 days' worth	☐	☐	☐
Peanut butter, granola bars, and so forth	3 days' worth	☐	☐	☐
Multivitamins	1 bottle each	☐	☐	☐
Foods for infants or people on special diets	7 days' worth	☐	☐	☐
Cookies and hard candy	1 box each	☐	☐	☐
Cereal	2 boxes	☐	☐	☐
Powdered milk	2 boxes	☐	☐	☐

CLOTHES AND BEDDING SUPPLIES

In a disaster, basic comforts can mean the difference between coping and breaking down. Do not forget to store bedding and clean clothes.

Table B.6
Emergency Clothes and Bedding

Supplies	Unit	Home kit
Complete change of clothes	3 days' worth	☐
Sturdy shoes or boots	1 pair	☐
Rain gear	1 set	☐
Hat and gloves	1 set	☐
Extra socks	3 pairs	☐
Extra underwear	3 pairs	☐
Thermal underwear	1 set	☐
Sunglasses	1 pair	☐
Blanket/sleeping bag and pillow	1 each	☐

VITAL INFORMATION

Also make sure that you keep these items in a watertight container. Consider using a fire-resistant safe to store these critical documents.

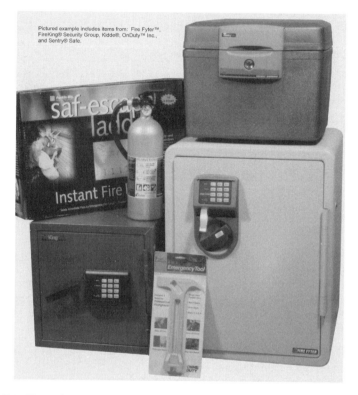

Figure B.3: Example Family Fire Equipment

Table B.7
Vital Information

Personal information	Unit	Home kit
Personal identification	1 each person	☐
Cash (small bills) and coins	$100	☐
Credit card	1 card	☐
Traveler's checks	$100	☐
Extra set of house keys and car keys	1 set	☐
Copy of birth certificate	1 each person	☐
Copy of marriage certificate	1 each	☐
Copy of driver's license	1 each person	☐
Copy of Social Security card	1 each person	☐
Copy of passport	1 each person	☐
Copy of will	1 each	☐
Copy of deed	1 each	☐
Copy of inventory of household goods	1 each	☐
Copy of insurance papers	1 each	☐
Copy of immunization records	1 each person	☐
Copy of bank and credit card account numbers	1 each	☐
Copy of stocks and bonds	1 each	☐
Emergency contact list and phone numbers	1 each	☐
Map of the area (highlight evacuation routes)	1 each	☐
Evacuation route turn-by-turn directions	1 each	☐
List of phone numbers of places to stay	1 each	☐

APPENDIX C

First Aid in an NBC Environment

GENERAL

Include a comprehensive first-aid manual in your disaster supplies kit. This appendix provides special information about nuclear, biological, and chemical (NBC) threats because it is not likely that a standard first-aid manual will include guidelines for handling NBC emergencies. In any medical emergency (including an NBC crisis), always remember the basics of first aid:

- Check for *breathing*—Lack of oxygen intake (through a compromised airway or inadequate breathing) can lead to brain damage or death in just a few minutes.
- Check for *bleeding*—Life cannot continue without an adequate volume of blood to carry oxygen to tissues.
- Treat for *shock*—Unless shock is prevented, first aid performed, and medical treatment provided, death may result even though the injury would not otherwise be fatal.
- Send for *help*—When you observe an unconscious or ill, injured, or wounded person, you must carefully evaluate the casualty to determine the first-aid measures required to prevent further injury or death. You should seek help from medical personnel as soon as possible, but you must not interrupt your evaluation of the casualty or fail to administer first-aid measures. If possible, send somebody else to find medical help.

NBC First-Aid Materials

Consider joining your local Volunteer First-Aid Squad, Volunteer Fire Department, or Community Emergency Response Team (CERT). Members of these organizations may receive first-responder training and access to specialized equipment in the event of an emergency, including NBC protective overgarments, gas masks, and NBC first-aid supplies. In the event of a terrorist NBC attack, responding authorities may issue one or more specialized materials developed for use by the U.S. military to protect, decontaminate, and use as first aid for NBC exposure. You should know how to use the items; some items are described below. It is equally important that you know when to use them. Most likely, authorities will issue these items to first responders and other emergency personnel before issuing them to the general public.

- **Nerve Agent Pyridostigmine Pretreatment (NAPP)**—If authorities determine that the threat of a nerve agent attack is imminent, you may be issued a blister pack of pretreatment tablets. The NAPP is a pretreatment; it is not an antidote. It improves the effectiveness of the nerve agent antidote. When ordered to take the pretreatment you must take one tablet every 8 hours. This must be taken prior to exposure to nerve agents, since it may take several hours to develop adequate blood levels.
- **M291 Skin Decontaminating Kit**—The M291 Skin Decontaminating Kit contains six packets of XE-555 decontaminant resin.

   WARNING: For external use only. May be slightly irritating to the eyes. Keep decontaminating powder out of eyes. Use water to wash toxic agent out of eyes.

- **Nerve Agent Antidote Kit, MARK I**—First aid for nerve agent poisoning.
- **Antidote Treatment, Nerve Agent, Autoinjector (ATNAA)**—An alternative to the MARK I kit, the ATNAA is a multichambered device with the atropine and pralidoxime chloride in separate chambers. Both antidotes will be administered through a single needle.
- **Potassium Iodide (KI)**—If authorities determine that the threat of a so-called dirty bomb or Radiological Dispersion Device (RDD) attack is imminent (or has already occurred), you may be issued a blister pack of KI tablets. The KI is a protective treatment. Potassium iodide is a compound that may be used during a radiological emergency to protect against thyroid cancer caused by exposure to radioactive iodine. This should be taken prior to exposure to radiation, since it may take time to develop adequate blood levels and reach the thyroid. KI is also available to the public without a prescription.
- **Personal Protective Equipment (PPE)**—Special clothing (usually charcoal-lined jacket and pants/coveralls or long-sleeved fluid-resistant gowns/coveralls/suits) including rubber boots, rubber gloves, a field protective mask, and a hood.

Classification of Chemical and Biological Agents

Chemical agents are classified according to the primary physiological effects they produce, such as blistering, choking, vomiting, and incapacitating agents. Chemical agents are commonly dispersed using munitions or aerodynamic dissemination from a low-flying aircraft. Note that effective dispersion is very difficult and highly dependent upon wind direction and other atmospheric conditions.

Biological warfare agents are classified according to the effect they have on humans. The effects include their ability to incapacitate and cause death. Most biological warfare agents are delivered as aerosols that affect the respiratory tract; some can be delivered by releasing infected insects, by contaminating food and water, and by injection (injecting material in individuals via a terrorist, not mass exposure). These agents are found in living organisms such as fungi, bacteria, and viruses.

> **WARNING:** Swallowing water or food contaminated with nerve, blister, and other chemical agents and with some biological agents can be fatal. *Never* consume water or food that is suspected of being contaminated until it has been tested and found safe for consumption by medical personnel.

Conditions that May Signal a Chemical or Biological Attack

Once an attack with a chemical or biological agent is detected or suspected, or information is available that such an agent is about to be used, you must *immediately* evacuate to a prepared safe room or protected location. *Do not wait* to receive an order or alarm from authorities under these circumstances:

- Explosions that produce vapors, smoke, and mists, and aerial sprays.
- Smoke or vapor cloud from an unknown source is present or approaching.
- A suspicious odor, liquid, or solid is present.
- A chemical or biological warfare agent attack is occurring.
- When casualties are being received from an area where chemical or biological agents have reportedly been used.
- You have one or more symptoms:

  —An unexplained runny nose
  —A sudden unexplained headache
  —A feeling of choking or tightness in the chest or throat
  —Dimness of vision
  —Irritation of the eyes
  —Difficulty in or increased rate of breathing without obvious reasons
  —Sudden feeling of depression
  —Dread, anxiety, or restlessness
  —Dizziness or light-headedness
  —Slurred speech
  —Unexplained laughter or unusual behavior in others
  —Numerous unexplained ill personnel

—Others suddenly collapsing without evident cause

—Animals or birds exhibiting unusual behavior or suddenly dying

FIRST AID FOR A CHEMICAL ATTACK

- A field protective mask gives protection against biological and chemical warfare agents as well as radiological fallout. If you don't have access to a mask, promptly evacuate to a safe room or protected location.

- If symptoms of nerve agent poisoning appear, immediately give yourself one MARK I or ATNAA.

    CAUTION: *Do not* inject a nerve agent antidote until you are sure you need it.

- If your eyes and face become contaminated, you must immediately try to get under cover. You need shelter to prevent further contamination while performing decontamination procedures on your face. If no overhead cover is available, cover your head with an article of clothing before beginning the decontamination process. Then put on the remaining protective clothing (or a clean change of clothing). Decontaminate (if no decontamination kits are available, use soap and water to thoroughly remove contaminants) outside your protected area or safe room before entering.

- If nerve agents are used, personal safety permitting, watch for persons needing nerve agent antidotes.

- Decontaminate your skin immediately, and clothing as soon as possible.

NERVE AGENTS

Nerve agents are among the deadliest of chemical agents. Nerve agents enter the body by inhalation, by ingestion, and through the skin. Sarin, Soman, Tabun and VX are the primary agents in this group. Depending on the route of entry and the amount, nerve agents can produce injury or death within minutes. Nerve agents can achieve their effects with small amounts. Nerve agents are absorbed rapidly, and the effects are felt immediately upon entry into the body. You may be issued three MARK I kits or three ATNAA kits and one Convulsant Antidote for Nerve Agent (CANA). Each MARK I kit consists of one atropine autoinjector and one pralidoxime chloride (2 PAM Cl) autoinjector. Each ATNAA kit consists of a multichambered autoinjector with the atropine and pralidoxime chloride in separate chambers. The CANA is a single autoinjector with flanges. Procedures for use of both the MARK I and ATNAA are described below. You will use either the MARK I or the ATNAA.

When you perceive the signs and symptoms of nerve agent poisoning, you should immediately put on the protective mask (if available) and then inject yourself with one set of the MARK I or ATNAA. *Do not* administer the CANA. You should inject yourself in the outer (lateral) thigh muscle, or if you are thin, in the upper outer (lateral) part of the buttocks.

Signs and Symptoms of Nerve Agent Poisoning

The symptoms of nerve agent poisoning are grouped as *mild*—those that you recognize and for which you can perform self-aid—and *severe*—those which require assistance from medical personnel.

Mild Signs and Symptoms:

• Unexplained runny nose
• Unexplained sudden headache
• Sudden drooling
• Difficulty seeing (dimness of vision and miosis)
• Tightness in the chest or difficulty in breathing
• Localized sweating and muscular twitching in the area of contaminated skin
• Stomach cramps
• Nausea
• Tachycardia followed by bradycardia. (Tachycardia is an abnormally rapid heartbeat with a heart rate of over 100 beats per minute. Bradycardia is a slow heart rate of less than 60 beats per minute.)

Severe Signs and Symptoms:

• Strange or confused behavior
• Wheezing, dyspnea (difficulty in breathing), and coughing
• Severely pinpointed pupils
• Red eyes with tearing
• Vomiting
• Severe muscular twitching and general weakness
• Involuntary urination and defecation
• Convulsions
• Unconsciousness
• Respiratory failure
• Bradycardia

First Aid for Nerve Agent Poisoning

First aid for nerve agent poisoning consists of administering the MARK I or ATNAA and CANA. The injection site for administering the antidotes is normally in the outer thigh muscle. The thigh injection site is the area about a hand's width above the knee to a hand's width below the hip joint. It is important that the injection be given into a large muscle area. If the individual is thinly built, then the injections should be administered into the upper outer quarter (quadrant) of the buttock. Injecting in the buttocks of a thinly built individual avoids injury to the thighbone.

Self-administer MARK I. If you experience any or all of the nerve agent *mild* symptoms, you must *immediately* put on your protective mask (or promptly evacuate to a safe room) and self-administer one MARK I, as follows:

1. Obtain one mark i (or atnaa) kit.
2. Check injection site.
3. For mark i kit, remove the atropine injector (the smaller injector of the pair). For atnaa kit, remove safety clip from the single injector.
4. Clear hard objects from injection site (check pockets for interfering objects).
5. For mark i kit, inject atropine (smaller device) at injection site, applying even pressure to the injector. For atnaa kit, inject atnaa (single device) at injection site, applying even pressure to the injector.
6. You must hold autoinjectors in place for 10 seconds.
7. Hold used autoinjector with nondominant hand. Bend needle of used injector by pressing on a hard surface to form a hook.
8. For mark i kit, now remove the larger injector containing Protopam Chloride or 2-PAM Chloride (2 pam cl), inject (larger device) at site, applying even pressure to the injector for 10 seconds, and then bend needle of the used injector by pressing on a hard surface to form a hook.
9. Attach used injector(s) with bent needles to shirt pocket flap or collar.
10. Massage injection site.
11. Seek medical attention.

CAUTION: *Do not* use your own MARK I, ATNAA, or CANA on a casualty. If you use your own, you may not have any antidote if needed for self-aid.

WARNINGS:

- Only administer one MARK I or ATNAA as self-aid. *Do not* self-administer CANA.
- *Do not* cover or hold the needle end with your hand, thumb, or fingers—you might accidentally inject yourself. An accidental injection into the hand *will not* deliver an effective dose of the antidote, especially if the needle goes through the hand.
- If you are thinly built, inject yourself into the upper outer quadrant of the buttock. There is a nerve that crosses the buttocks; hitting this nerve can cause paralysis. Therefore, you must only inject into the upper outer quadrant of the buttock. *Do not* inject into areas close to the hip, knee, or thighbone.
- *Do not* give yourself another set of injections. If you are able to walk without assistance, know who you are, and where you are, you *will not* need the second set of injections. (If not needed, giving yourself a second set of MARK I injections or ATNAA may create a nerve agent antidote overdose, which could cause incapacitation.)
- When masking a casualty or administering the nerve agent antidotes to a casualty, squat but *do not* kneel. Kneeling may force any chemical agent on your overgarment into or through your protective clothing.

- If medical personnel are not available, and if you (or a casualty) have received the initial three sets of MARK I, then you may administer additional atropine injections at approximately 15-minute intervals until atropinization is achieved (i.e., a heart rate above 90 beats per minute, reduced bronchial secretions, and reduced salivations).

- Administer additional atropine at intervals of 30 minutes to 4 hours to maintain atropinization or until you (or a casualty) are placed under the care of medical personnel. Check the heart rate by lifting the casualty's mask hood and feeling for a pulse at the carotid artery. You must locate medical assistance as soon as possible.

- If medical personnel are not available, you may have to administer CANA to casualties suffering convulsions. Administer a second, and if needed, a third CANA at 5 to 10 minute intervals for a maximum of three injections (30 milligrams diazepam). Follow the steps and procedures described for administering auto injectors. *Do not* give more than two additional injections for a total of three.

BLISTER AGENTS

Blister agents (vesicants) include mustard (H and HD), nitrogen mustards (HN), lewisite (L), and other arsenicals, mixtures of mustards and arsenicals, and phosgene oxime (CX). Blister agents may act on the eyes, mucous membranes, lungs, and skin. They burn and blister the skin or any other body parts they contact. Even relatively low doses may cause serious injury.

Blister agents damage the respiratory tract (nose, sinuses, and windpipe) when inhaled and cause vomiting and diarrhea when absorbed. Lewisite and CX cause immediate pain on contact. However, mustard agents are deceptive as there is little or no pain at the time of exposure. Thus, in some cases, signs of injury may not appear for several hours after exposure.

Protective Measures

Your protective mask with hood and protective overgarment provide protection against blister agents. If it is known or suspected that blister agents are being used, *stop breathing*, and put on your mask and your protective overgarment.

> **CAUTION:** Large drops of liquid vesicants on the protective overgarment ensemble may penetrate it if allowed to stand for an extended period. Remove large drops as soon as possible.

Signs and Symptoms of Blister Agent Poisoning

- Immediate and intense pain upon contact with L, LH (lewisite and mustard) mixture, and CX. No initial pain upon contact with mustard.

- Inflammation and blisters (burns) resulting in tissue destruction. The severity of a chemical burn is directly related to the concentration of the agent and the duration of contact with the skin. The longer the agent is in contact with the tissue, the more serious the injury will be.

- Vomiting and diarrhea. Exposure to high concentrations of vesicants may cause vomiting or diarrhea.
- Death. The blister agent vapors absorbed during ordinary field exposure will probably not cause enough internal body (systemic) damage to result in death. However, death may occur from prolonged exposure to high concentrations of vapor or from extensive liquid contamination over wide areas of the skin, particularly when decontamination is neglected or delayed.

First-Aid Measures for Blister Agent Poisoning

- Use your M291 Skin Decontaminating Kit to decontaminate your skin, and use water to flush contaminated eyes. Decontamination of vesicants must be done immediately (within 1 minute is best).
- If blisters form, cover them loosely with a field dressing, and secure the dressing.

> **CAUTION:** Blisters are actually burns. *Do not* attempt to decontaminate the skin where blisters have formed, as the agent has already been absorbed.

- If you receive blisters over a wide area of the body, you are considered seriously burned. Seek medical assistance immediately.
- Remember, if vomiting or diarrhea occurs after having been exposed to blister agents, seek medical assistance immediately.

CHOKING AGENTS (LUNG-DAMAGING AGENTS)

Chemical agents that attack lung tissue, primarily causing fluid buildup (pulmonary edema), are classified as choking agents (lung-damaging agents). This group includes phosgene (CG), diphosgene (DP), chlorine (Cl), and chloropicrin (PS). Of these four agents, CG is the most dangerous and is more likely to be employed by the enemy in future conflicts.

Protective Measures

A field protective mask gives adequate protection against choking agents. Generally, first responders and emergency service personnel have access to field protective masks. Contact your local Office of Emergency Management to find out if they are prepared to supply the public in the event of an attack. Consider procuring masks for your family from a reputable supplier and be aware of the filter expiration dates.

Signs and Symptoms of Choking Agents

During and immediately after exposure to choking agents (depending on agent concentration and length of exposure), you may experience some or all of these signs and symptoms:

- Tears (lacrimation)
- Coughing
- Choking
- Tightness of chest
- Nausea and vomiting
- Headaches

Self-Aid

The protective mask should be put on immediately when any of the conditions described above exist. Another indication of a CG attack is an odor like newly mown hay; however, *do not* rely on odor as indication of a chemical attack.

If some CG is inhaled, conserve your energy but evacuate the area and seek medical assistance unless you experience difficulty in breathing, nausea, vomiting, or more than the usual shortness of breath during exertion. If any of the above symptoms occur, remain at quiet rest until medical evacuation is accomplished.

With ordinary field exposure to choking agents, death will probably not occur. However, prolonged exposure to high concentrations of the vapor and neglect or delay in masking can be fatal.

CYANOGEN (BLOOD) AGENTS

Cyanogen agents interfere with proper oxygen utilization in the body. Hydrogen cyanide (AC) and cyanogen chloride (CK) are the primary agents in this group.

Protective Measures

Your protective mask with a fresh filter gives adequate protection against field concentrations of cyanogen agent vapor. The protective overgarments, as well as the mask, are needed when exposed to liquid AC.

Signs and Symptoms of Cyanogen Agent Poisoning

During and immediately after exposure to cyanogen agents (depending on agent concentration and length of exposure), you may experience some or all of these signs and symptoms:

- Tearing (lacrimation)
- Eye, nose, and throat irritation
- Sudden stimulation of breathing (unable to hold breath)

- Nausea
- Coughing
- Tightness of chest
- Headache
- Light-headedness (dizziness)
- Unconsciousness

First Aid for Cyanogen Agent Poisoning

If you suspect that you have been exposed to blood agents, seek medical assistance immediately. Do not hesitate as Cyanogen agents act *very* quickly to deprive your body of oxygen. Typically, two forms of Cyanogen agents are used in attacks:

Hydrogen Cyanide

During any chemical attack, if you get a sudden stimulation of breath or detect an odor like bitter almonds, *put on your mask immediately*. Speed is absolutely essential since this agent acts so rapidly that within a few seconds, its effects will make it impossible for you to put on your mask by yourself. Stop breathing until the mask is on, if at all possible. This may be very difficult since the agent strongly stimulates respiration.

Cyanogen Chloride

Put your mask on immediately if you experience any irritation of the eyes, nose, or throat.

INCAPACITATING AGENTS AND FIRST AID

An incapacitating agent is a chemical agent that produces temporary, disabling conditions that persist for hours to days after exposure. Unlike riot-control agents, which usually are momentary or fleeting in action, incapacitating agents have a persistent effect. It is likely that smoke-producing munitions or aerosols will disseminate such agents, thus making breathing their means of entry into the body. The protective mask is, therefore, essential.

There are no specific first-aid measures to relieve the symptoms of incapacitating agents. Supportive first aid and physical restraint may be indicated. If the casualty is stuporous or comatose, be sure that respiration is unobstructed; then turn him on his or her side in case vomiting should occur. Complete cleansing of the skin with soap and water should be done as soon as possible, or the M291 Skin Decontaminating Kit can be used if washing is impossible. Remove weapons and other potentially harmful items from victims who are suspected of having these symptoms. Harmful items include cigarettes, matches, medications, and small items that might be swallowed accidentally. Delirious (confused) persons have been known to attempt to eat items bearing only a superficial resemblance to food.

Incapacitating agents (anticholinergic drugs BZ type) may produce alarming dryness and coating of the lips and tongue; however, there is usually no danger of immediate dehydration. Fluids should be given sparingly, if at all, because of the danger of vomiting and because of the likelihood of temporary urinary retention due to paralysis of bladder muscles.

If the body temperature is elevated and mucous membranes are dry, immediate and vigorous cooling (as for heatstroke) is indicated. Methods that can be used to cool the skin are spraying with cool water and air circulation (fanning); applying alcohol soaked cloths and air circulation; and providing maximum exposure to air in a shaded area, along with maximum air circulation. Such cases are usually a result of anticholinergic poisoning. Rapid evacuation should be accomplished since medical treatment with the appropriate medication may be lifesaving.

CAUTION: *Do not* use ice for cooling the skin. Long-term exposure to ice can potentially cause tissue damage.

Reassurance and a firm but friendly attitude by individuals providing first aid will be beneficial if the casualty appears to comprehend what is being said. Conversation is a waste of time if the victim is incoherent or cannot understand what is being said. In such cases, the less said, the better—these casualties will benefit more from prompt and vigorous restraint and evacuation to a medical facility.

INCENDIARY AGENTS AND FIRST AID

Incendiaries can be grouped as white phosphorous (WP), thickened gasoline, metal, and oil and metal. You must learn to protect yourself against these incendiaries.

White phosphorus is used primarily as a smoke producer but can be used for its incendiary effect to ignite field expedients and combustible materials. The burns from WP are usually multiple, deep, and variable in size. When particles of WP get on the skin or clothing, they continue to burn until deprived of air. They also have a tendency to stick to a surface and must be brushed off or picked out.

- If burning particles of WP strike and stick to your clothing, quickly take off the contaminated clothing before the WP burns through to the skin.
- If burning WP strikes your skin, smother the flame with water, a wet cloth, or mud.

NOTE: Since WP is soluble in oil, *do not* use grease, oily ointments, or eye ointments to smother the flame.

- Keep the WP particles covered with a wet material to exclude air until you can remove them or have them removed from your skin.
- Remove the WP particles from the skin by brushing them with a wet cloth and by picking them out with a knife, stick, or other available object.
- Seek medical assistance as soon as possible.

Thickened fuel mixtures (napalm) have a tendency to cling to clothing and body surfaces, thereby producing prolonged exposure and severe burns. The first aid for these burns is the same as for other heat burns. The heat and irritating gases given off by these combustible mixtures may cause lung damage, which must be treated by medical personnel.

Metal incendiaries pose special problems. Thermite particles on the skin should be immediately cooled with water and then removed. The first aid for these burns is the same as for other heat burns. Particles of magnesium on the skin burn quickly and deeply. Like other metal incendiaries, they must be removed. Ordinarily, medical personnel should do the complete removal of these particles as soon as possible. Immediate medical treatment is required.

Oil and metal incendiaries have much the same effect on contact with the skin and clothing as those discussed above.

BIOLOGICAL AGENTS AND FIRST AID

Biological agents are disease-causing organisms introduced into a population. Anthrax, plague, and smallpox are some of the diseases included in this group.

Once a disease is identified, first aid or medical treatment is initiated, depending on the seriousness of the disease. First-aid measures are concerned with observable symptoms of the disease such as diarrhea or vomiting.

TOXINS

Toxins are alleged to have been used in past terrorist attacks. Witnesses and victims have described the agent as toxic rain (or yellow rain) because it was reported to have been released from aircraft as a yellow powder or liquid that covered ground, structures, vegetation, and people.

Signs and Symptoms of Toxin Exposure

The occurrence of the symptoms from toxins may appear in a period of a few minutes to several hours depending on the particular toxin, the person's susceptibility, and the amount of toxin inhaled, ingested, or deposited on the skin. Symptoms from toxins usually involve the central nervous system but are often preceded by less prominent symptoms, such as nausea, vomiting, diarrhea, cramps, or stomach irritation and a burning sensation. Typical neurological symptoms often develop rapidly in severe cases; for example, visual disturbances, inability to swallow, speech difficulty, lack of muscle coordination, and sensory abnormalities (numbness of mouth, throat, or extremities). Yellow rain (mycotoxins) also may have hemorrhagic symptoms, which could include the following:

- Dizziness
- Severe itching or tingling of the skin
- Formation of multiple small, hard blisters
- Coughing up blood
- Shock (which could result in death)

Self-Aid for Toxin Exposure

Upon recognition of an attack employing toxins, you must immediately do the following:

- Stop breathing, put on your protective mask with hood, and then resume breathing. Next, put on your protective clothing.
- Should severe itching of the face become unbearable, quickly take these steps:
  —Locate fresh water (not standing water that may have been contaminated).
  —Take and hold a deep breath, and lift your mask.
  —While holding your breath, close your eyes and flush your face with generous amounts of water.

  CAUTION: *Do not* rub or scratch your eyes. Try not to let the water run onto your clothing or protective overgarment.

  —Put your protective mask back on, seat it properly, clear it, and check it for a seal; then resume breathing.
  —Decontaminate your skin by bathing with soap and water as soon as possible.
- Change clothing and decontaminate your protective mask using soap and water. Replace the filters if directed.
- If you suspect that you have been exposed to toxins, you should seek medical assistance immediately.

NUCLEAR DETONATION, RDD EVENTS, OR NUCLEAR REACTOR ACCIDENTS

Three types of injuries may result from a nuclear detonation. These are thermal, blast, and radiation injuries. Many times, the casualty will have a combination of these types of injuries. Provide first aid for thermal and blast injuries based on observable injuries, such as burns, hemorrhage, or fractures.

The signs and symptoms of radiation illness in the initial phase include the rapid onset of nausea, vomiting, and malaise (tiredness). The only first-aid procedure for radiological casualties is decontamination.

Potassium iodide (KI) is a compound that may be used in the event of a radiological emergency to protect against thyroid cancer caused by exposure to radioactive iodine. KI is a safe and effective nonprescription medication approved by the FDA. KI blocks the uptake of radioactive iodine by the thyroid gland. KI does not protect a person or the thyroid from direct exposure to radiation that may be released in the event of a radiological emergency. Taking KI will only saturate the thyroid with nonradioactive iodine. Children under 14 years of age are most at risk from the effects of radioactive iodine on the thyroid gland. To be most effective, KI should be taken before or immediately after exposure to radioactive iodine.

KI may not be safe for people with existing thyroid conditions or an allergy to iodine. You should consult your physician before you consider using KI as a protective measure. Also, follow the manufacturer's directions for storage and use.

Appendix D

Disaster Planning for Pets and Livestock

GENERAL

In the event of a disaster, most communities will be prepared to open shelters for you and your family. However, for public health and safety reasons, pets are not usually allowed to enter these shelters. It is your personal obligation to plan for your pet's emergency needs. Research ahead of time where to find local shelter for your pets, and if none exists, consider organizing a place in your community.

It's important to note that historically, some pet owners have made themselves a public health risk because they failed to plan for their pets' safety and refused to leave their homes when faced with a disaster. When people won't evacuate as directed by local authorities, emergency personnel must often put their lives in peril to respond to the additional complications that result.

PLANNING FOR DOMESTIC PETS

Before a Disaster

- **Plan Ahead**—In the event of an evacuation, pets may not be allowed inside human emergency shelters. Determine the best place to leave your pet in case of a disaster. Identify an off-site location as well as a place in your home.

- **Keep Current Identification and Photographs**—Dogs and cats should always wear properly fitting collars and personal identification, rabies, and license tags. Make sure all the information on the tags is current. Keep a current photo of each pet. Make sure any distinguishing markings are visible. Birds should be leg-banded. You will need proof of ownership to retrieve your pet from a shelter. Consider including additional contact information *for a relative or friend outside your area* on your pet's identification tags.

- **Maintain Disaster Preparation Kits**—You should prepare a kit for each of your pets. Consider these items:
  - Portable radio and extra batteries
  - Rugged transportable cage (large enough to stand up and turn around)
  - Cage cover or blanket
  - Cat litter and a box
  - Nonspill food and water bowls or dispensers
  - At least three days' supply of food and water
  - Any special dietary instructions and medicines and dosages
  - Collars, leashes, harnesses, and/or soft muzzles
  - Hot-water bottle
  - Newspaper or cage liner
  - First-aid items
  - Paper towels and plastic bags
  - Disinfectants
  - Toys and treats
  - For snakes and reptiles, water bowl for soaking and a heating pad
  - Battery powered heat lamp
  - Veterinarian's information
  - List of emergency contacts and telephone numbers
  - List of local animal shelters
  - Current photograph of each pet
  - Articles with your scent and your pet's scent
  - Copies of relief plans developed by your local Red Cross chapter; emergency management office; or police, fire, health, wildlife, and agriculture departments

- **Store Important Animal Documents**—These should include vaccination and medical records. Keep these documents in a ziplock or waterproof plastic bag (and consider securing them in a fireproof/waterproof safe). Keep medical histories, and record special dosing instructions and dietary requirements. Write down contact information for your veterinarian.

- **Vaccinate Your Pets**—Your pets need to be current on vaccinations. You will be required to show proof of vaccination if you need to board your pet.

- **Plan for Transportation**—Each animal should have its own airline-approved pet carrier. Normal cages may not be sturdy enough to hold your pet during a disaster. Familiarize your pet with the carrier or cage before an emergency. Label the carrier with your name and contact information.

- **Secure Aquariums**—Fish tanks and aquariums are very top heavy and unstable. They should be secured or bolted to wall studs or placed on the floor to prevent them from toppling. Consider keeping a smaller fishbowl or lidded container handy for transporting fish or reptiles temporarily.

- **Have Leashes and Collars**—Keep a leash handy for each dog and cat in your home. Consider using a harness and/or soft muzzle.

- **Set Up a Buddy System**—In case you are not home when disaster strikes, ask a trusted neighbor to check on your animals. Exchange veterinary information, and file a permission slip with your veterinarian authorizing that neighbor to get emergency treatment for your pet if you can't be located.

During a Disaster

If possible, take your pet with you when you evacuate. Use the guidelines below to provide for your pet's safety.

If You Take Your Pet

- If possible, evacuate your pet(s) early.
- Take your disaster preparedness kit, the pet's vaccination and medical records, and pet identification photographs with you.
- Bring enough pet food and water to last for at least three days.
- Monitor the Emergency Broadcast System on the television or radio. Authorities may provide the locations of local temporary animal shelters.
- Call your destination to make sure that space is still available.
- In cold weather, if time permits, wrap a blanket around the carrier and warm up the car before placing animals inside.
- You can transport snakes and reptiles in a pillowcase, but you must transfer them to more secure housing when you reach shelter.
- Keep birds caged. They may sense danger and pose an uncharacteristic flight risk.

If You Cannot Take Your Pet

- Bring your pet indoors. Do not leave pets chained outdoors.
- Prepare a preselected site indoors for your pet. Use a room with no windows but adequate ventilation, such as a utility room, garage, bathroom, or other area that can be easily cleaned. Do not tie pets up. Depending on the nature of the emergency, consider a location on an upper floor of your home.
- Leave only dry food and fresh water in nonspill containers. If possible, open a faucet to let water drip into a large container, or partially fill a bathtub with water.
- Do not leave vitamin treats (they could be fatal if overeaten).
- House cats and dogs separately, even if they normally get along.
- Cover bird cages with a light cloth or sheet to reduce stress and protect your pet from light debris.
- Do not rely on electric filters, feeding systems, or other electric equipment during a disaster.
- Turn off the power and gas.
- Take your pet's vaccination and medical records, and pet identification photographs with you when you depart.

After a Disaster

- **Monitor Your Pet(s)**—Pet behavior may change after an emergency. Watch your pets closely and keep them leashed. Familiar scents and landmarks may be altered or pets may be injured, both of which may cause confusion and abnormal behavior. Check animals for injury and exposure to chemicals. Contact your veterinarian if you have any concerns. Monitor birds closely for several days after a disaster. Many commonly show signs of disease several days after a stressful episode. Consult a veterinarian immediately at any signs of lethargy, loss of appetite, loose stool, depression, injury, or sitting on the bottom of the cage.

- **Be Aware of Dangers**—Watch for downed power lines, fallen trees, debris, and local wildlife that may pose a threat to you and your pet.

- **Acclimate Your Pets Slowly**—If you must move to new surroundings, do not remove your pet from its carrier until it is calm; then do so only in a closed room. Frightened animals may become aggressive or flee. If your pet has been without food and water for a prolonged time, give it small amounts every few hours for several days. Allowing the animal to gorge can be harmful. Work up to a normal volume of food gradually. Let your pet have plenty of uninterrupted sleep to recover from the stress and trauma. Birds will usually remain calm in isolated, darkened areas with cages covered.

- **If You Find a Pet**—Call Animal Control or any emergency phone numbers set up after the disaster. Isolate the found pet from your animals until it is returned to its owner or can be examined by a veterinarian.

  WARNING: A strange animal in a stressful situation may pose a threat to you, your family, and your pets. Do not take unnecessary risks.

- **Stay Informed about Disease Threats**—Check with your veterinarian and the state emergency management office for information about possible disease outbreaks in animals.

If You Have Lost Your Pet

- Visit each shelter in your area at least once every other day. You must check the shelter in person; you are the only person who can truly identify your animal. Keep a current photo of your pet showing or describing any distinctive markings.

- Create a flyer with your pet's photo, description, and name, as well as your name and phone numbers where you can be reached.

- When you do find your pet, immediately examine it for illness or injuries. Obtain medical attention from your veterinarian if needed. Use caution when handling animals. Panicky or injured animals may bite (even if they've never exhibited aggressive behavior before).

PLANNING FOR HORSES, LARGE ANIMALS, AND LIVESTOCK

Before a Disaster

- **Plan Ahead**—Determine the best place for animal confinement in case of a disaster. Find alternate water sources in case of a power outage (electric pumps will not work). Consider installing a backup manual pump. You should have a minimum of three days' feed and water on hand.

- **Keep Current Identification Records**—Photograph, identify, and inventory your horses. Permanent identification methods, including tattoos, brands, etched hooves or microchips, are best. Temporary identification, such as tags on halters, neck bands, and duct tape with permanent writing, will suffice on short notice. Include your name and phone number. Keep identification information with you to verify ownership. (Breed registration papers may already include this information.)

- **Store Important Animal Documents**—These should include vaccination and medical records. Keep these documents in a ziplock or waterproof plastic bag (and consider securing them in a fireproof/waterproof safe). Keep medical histories, and record special dosing instructions, allergies, and dietary requirements. Write down contact information for your veterinarian.

- **Vaccinate Your Horses**—Your horses need to be current on vaccinations. You may be required to show proof of vaccination if you need to stable your horses.

- **Plan for Transportation**—Decide where to take your animals if evacuation is necessary. Contact show grounds, fairgrounds, equestrian centers, private farms, and stables (outside of your immediate area) about their policies and ability to temporarily take in horses in an emergency. Be prepared with several sites, and call your destination before departure to make sure that space is still available. Familiarize yourself with multiple evacuation routes to your destination, and try to avoid routes used for mass evacuation. Keep trailers and vans well maintained, full of gas, and ready to move at all times. Be sure your animals will load (train them to board your trailers). If you don't have your own vehicles, make arrangements with local companies or neighbors before disaster strikes.

- **Maintain an Emergency Evacuation Kit**—You should prepare an emergency evacuation kit and keep it readily accessible (your trailer would be an ideal place). Consider including these items:
  - Portable radio and extra batteries
  - Two buckets (for food and water) for each horse
  - At least three days' supply of feed (hay and grain)
  - At least three days' supply of water (about 40 gallons, or about 150 liters, for each horse)
  - Specially designed, watertight plastic saddle stands for hauling water
  - Any special dietary instructions and medicines and dosages
  - At least three days' supply of any medications
  - Non-nylon halters, lead ropes, and shanks for each horse
  - Leg wraps
  - Horse blanket
  - Hoof pick
  - Plastic trash barrel with a lid
  - Shovel
  - Lyme or bleach
  - Wire cutters

- First-aid items
- Veterinarian's information
- List of emergency contacts and telephone numbers
- Registration papers and health records (including a negative Coggins)
- Current photographs of each horse
- Identification tags with your contact information for each horse
- Copies of relief plans developed by your local Red Cross chapter; emergency management office; or police, fire, health, wildlife, and agriculture departments

- **Set Up a Buddy System**—Work with your trusted neighbors. Exchange veterinary information, and file a permission slip with your veterinarian authorizing that neighbor to get emergency treatment for your horse(s) if you can't be located. Put your disaster plans in writing, and give copies to your family, neighbors, and barn helpers so that they will know what to do if disaster threatens when you are not around. Post emergency contact numbers at your barn.
- **Prepare for Fire Hazards**—In high-risk areas, clear firebreaks around your house, barns, and property lines. Keep firefighting tools in one location.

During a Disaster

If You Must Evacuate Your Horses

- If possible, evacuate your horses early and allow extra time for hauling.
- Take your emergency evacuation kit, the horses' vaccination and medical records, and individual horse identification photographs with you.
- Bring enough hay, grain, and water to last for at least three days (the average adult horse drinks 12+ gallons, or about 45+ liters, of water each day).
- Monitor the Emergency Broadcast System on the television or radio.
- Call your destination to make sure that space is still available.
- When you transport your horses, try to use roads not in use for human evacuation.

If You Cannot Evacuate Your Horses (or if Moving Them Would Be More Dangerous than Securing Them at Home)

- Move your horses to a preselected site appropriate to the threat (for example, seek higher ground to protect your horses from flooding). Do not tie them up if it is not necessary. If appropriate, consider turning out your horses into a safely fenced pasture with shelter (barns can be fire hazards in a disaster situation). Close the barn doors to prevent panicked horses from running back inside.
- Leave enough hay and grain to last for at least three days.
- Do not rely on automatic watering systems or other electric equipment during a disaster. Fill several clean drums with drinking water (the average adult horse drinks 12+ gallons, or about 45+ liters, of water each day).
- Turn off the power and gas.

- Take your horses' vaccination and medical records, and individual horse identification photographs with you when you depart.
- Note that the leading causes of death in large animals during disaster are the following:
  - Collapsed or burning barns
  - Kidney failure due to dehydration
  - Electrocution from downed power lines
  - Fencing failures

After a Disaster

- **Monitor Your Animals**—Check animals for injury and exposure to chemicals. Contact your veterinarian if you have any concerns.
- **Be Aware of Dangers**—Check fences to be sure that they are intact. Check pastures and fences for sharp objects that could injure horses. Watch for downed power lines, fallen trees, debris, and local wildlife that may pose a threat to you and your animals.
- **Acclimate Your Animals Slowly**—Familiar scents and landmarks may have changed, and animals can easily become confused and lost.
- **If You Find a Lost Animal**—Call Animal Control or any emergency phone numbers set up after the disaster. Isolate the lost animal from your animals until it is returned to its owner or can be examined by a veterinarian.

> **WARNING:** Always use caution when approaching and handling strange or frightened animals. Work in pairs and do not take unnecessary risks.

- **Stay Informed about Disease Threats**—Check with your veterinarian and the state emergency management office for information about possible disease outbreaks in large animals.

If You Have Lost an Animal

- Contact veterinarians, humane societies, stables, surrounding farms, and other facilities in your area at least once every other day. Keep current photographs of your horses showing or describing any distinctive markings.
- Monitor the Emergency Broadcast System on the television or radio. Authorities may provide the locations of local groups accepting lost animals.
- When you do find your horse, immediately examine it for illness or injuries. Obtain medical attention from your veterinarian if needed. Use caution when handling traumatized animals.

APPENDIX E

Evacuating Mass Transit

GENERAL

In the event of an emergency that requires the evacuation of a train, an airplane, or a bus, you can follow some simple guidelines to keep yourself safer. Remember that the best way to protect yourself is to remain calm, think clearly, and follow the instructions of the crew and attendants.

EMERGENCIES ON A TRAIN OR A SUBWAY CAR

- *Do Not* **Pull the Emergency Brake Cord**—Use the emergency brake cord only when the motion of the subway presents an imminent danger to life and limb. Otherwise, do not activate the emergency brake cord, especially in a tunnel. Once the emergency brake cord is pulled, the brakes have to be reset before the train can move again, which reduces the options for dealing with the emergency.

- **Stop**—Stay calm and do not immediately attempt to leave the train on your own. In most circumstances, leaving the train is more dangerous than staying put. Tracks may still be electrified, and other trains may still be in motion around you. If you cannot stay where you are, walk calmly to another car that is unaffected by the emergency. Do not try to leave the train without instructions or help from the train crew, other transit employees, and/or emergency services workers. Usually, the safest place for you is on the train.

- **Look**—If you see an emergency, find a member of the subway crew and report it immediately. The sooner trained personnel know about an emergency, the sooner they can act to bring the situation under control. On some cars, you can use two-way intercom systems (typically located at the ends of cars).

- **Listen**—It is important that you follow the instructions of subway/train crew members; other transit employees; and rescue, fire, or police personnel on the scene. The train crew will keep you informed about the emergency either in person or through the subway's public address system. Stay calm; in most instances, all that you need to do to be safe is to move to another car on the same train. If an evacuation is necessary, crew members, other transit employees, and emergency service workers will help you exit the train quickly and safely.

Types of Emergencies

Always notify subway/train crew members, and listen for announcements and instructions.

- **Fire or Smoke**
  - Notify the subway/train crew immediately.
  - If possible, move to another car through interior doors.
  - Assume that the tracks are electrified and remain inside.
  - Follow instructions from the subway/train crew and emergency personnel.
  - *Do not* pull the emergency brake cord.

- **Medical**
  - If a passenger is in distress, notify the subway/train crew immediately.
  - If you are qualified to assist, notify the subway/train crew.
  - Follow instructions from the subway/train crew and emergency personnel.
  - *Do not* pull the emergency brake cord.

- **Police**
  - Alert the subway/train crew to any unlawful or suspicious activity.
  - Subway/train crewmembers can notify the police en route.
  - *Do not* pull the emergency brake cord.

Before a Disaster

You should have a plan in case of an emergency and do your best to stay calm. Panicked passengers are likely to create bottlenecks at doorways. Passengers could be trampled in these situations. Know your alternate escape routes:

- Note where the emergency door or window release handles are located and how they operate.
- You can kick out windows labeled *Emergency* in one piece (without breaking), if the door release does not work.
- Read the emergency instructions posted in cars.

During a Disaster

Always notify subway/train crew members, and listen for announcements and instructions. The cars and interior ventilation systems on most modern subways and trains will protect passengers from many dangerous elements and conditions if they remain inside. Every system has emergency operating procedures in place where the operator, police, or other first responders will coordinate an evacuation, if necessary.

There are many hazards on the tracks, and passengers should never evacuate without instructions and assistance unless their lives are in imminent danger. You are likely safer remaining in the car, rather than evacuating. However, if it becomes necessary to evacuate the train, remember to listen to the instructions given by train crew members or other emergency responders who will tell you what to do. There are four ways that you may be evacuated from a train to a safe area:

- **Train to Benchwall**—Train crews and other emergency personnel will assist you to the area of the tracks adjacent to the train known as the *benchwall* and lead you to an emergency exit or station platform.
- **Transfer to a Train Ahead or Behind**—Train crews and other emergency personnel will assist you in transferring from the train you were riding (moving from car to car through interior doors) to another train that has pulled up ahead or behind.
- **Transfer to a Train Alongside**—Train crews and other emergency personnel will assist you from the train you were riding to another train that has pulled up alongside. A device will be placed to enable you to move directly into the other train. Crew members may direct you to move from car to car through interior doors to the car where the exit device is in place.
- **Evacuating to the Track Bed**—After attempting to remove power, train crews and other emergency personnel will assist you in evacuating to the track bed and lead you safely to an emergency exit or station platform. *Warning:* Always assume that the track is electrified, and avoid touching any part of the rail.

After a Disaster Evacuation

Just because you are off of the train does not mean that you can assume you are out of danger. As always, listen for announcements and instructions from subway/train crew members and emergency personnel. Additionally, follow these safety guidelines:

- **Walk into the Wind**—Most subway systems are designed to carry a natural air current that should carry toxins and smoke away from the incident. Additionally, if you walk toward the wind, you will be following the natural path of the tunnel toward station stops.
- **Do Not Touch the Rails**—If you must evacuate to the track bed, always walk down the center of the track bed (in between the two main rails). Most systems (including New York City) use a powered third rail. The third rail will almost always be the most interior rail (or the farthest from the tunnel walls). Authorities will attempt to remove power in the event of an emergency, but you should always assume that the track is electrified.

- **Be Aware of Oncoming Trains**—Authorities will attempt to remove power and shut down the system in the event of an emergency. However, you should assume nothing and maintain an awareness of your surroundings. If you see an oncoming train, quickly make your way to the nearest wall (while minding the third rail), and grasp any anchored object tightly. An oncoming train will create a vacuum that may pull you into its path as it approaches. Many systems have railings along most of their exterior walls to help.

- **Watch Your Step**—Tracks are difficult to navigate even when they are not obscured in smoke and possibly littered with wreckage and debris. Walk slowly, mind the third rail, stay low to maintain visibility in smoke, and take care to avoid injuring yourself. Keep moving until you safely reach an emergency exit or station platform.

EMERGENCIES ON A SCHOOL (OR COMMUTER) BUS

- **Stop**—Stay calm and do not immediately attempt to leave the bus on your own. In most circumstances, leaving the bus is more dangerous than staying put.

- **Look**—If you see fire or smoke, stay low to maintain visibility. Note the final resting position of the bus and its relationship to traffic and other hazards.

- **Listen**—It is important that you follow the instructions of the bus driver, a teacher, an aide, or emergency personnel on the scene. If an evacuation is necessary, the bus driver or emergency service workers will help you exit the bus quickly and safely.

Before a Disaster

You should have a plan in case of an emergency and do your best to stay calm. If an evacuation is necessary, you may only have about two to five minutes to escape without serious bodily injury.

Panicked passengers are likely to create bottlenecks at doorways and emergency exits. Passengers could be trampled in these situations. Know your alternate escape routes:

- Make sure that your school district conducts bus safety drills at least twice each year.
- Note where the emergency door or window release handles are located and how they operate.
- Look around and make a mental note of where the emergency exits are located. Know that some busses are also equipped with floor-level emergency exit doors. Count the number of seats to the nearest exit.
- Usually, you can kick out windows labeled *Emergency* in one piece (without breaking), if the door release does not work.
- Read the posted emergency instructions.
- Note where the fire extinguisher is located (usually at the front of the bus, near the driver), and consider how to remove it from the mounting bracket.
- Note where the first-aid kit is located (usually at the front of the bus, near the driver).

During a Disaster

A school bus (or a commuter bus) is a *very* safe means of transportation, and evacuations are very rarely necessary. However, emergencies do happen, and if it does become necessary to evacuate the bus, each passenger must know what to do. Remember to listen to the instructions given by the bus driver, a teacher, an aide, or emergency personnel who will tell you what to do. Additionally, follow these general rules:

- Remain seated and quiet until the bus is completely stopped. Do not change seats unless instructed to do so by the bus driver, a teacher, an aide, or emergency personnel.
- Face forward in the seat, and keep your hands, feet, and head away from the windows and inside the bus at all times.
- Be courteous to others, and pay attention to the bus driver, teacher, aide, and emergency personnel.
- When you are moving to the proper emergency exit, do not push or shove.
- While leaving the bus, use the handrails or the evacuation helpers' hands.
- Be on the lookout for traffic and pedestrians. Observe safety procedures while crossing the street.
- Be aware of debris and hazards around the bus and in your exit path. Look for downed power lines, hazardous material spills, leaking fuel, open flames, and so forth.
- Walk directly to a safe area (at least 40 to 50 paces away), and remain there with your group. Be sure to move upwind to avoid smoke.
- As always, children should not talk to strangers or accept rides from anyone.

After a Disaster Evacuation

Just because you are off of the bus does not mean that you can assume you are out of danger. As always, listen for instructions from the bus driver, teacher, aide, and emergency personnel. Additionally, follow these safety guidelines:

- **Stay Out of Danger Zones**—Move away from the front, sides, or back of the bus. These are all areas where you cannot be seen from inside. If the bus was moved while you were standing in one of these areas, you could be seriously injured or killed.
- **Be Aware of Oncoming Traffic**—Authorities will attempt to divert or halt traffic in the event of an emergency. However, you should assume nothing and maintain an awareness of your surroundings.
- **Watch Your Step**—The area around the bus may be obscured in smoke and possibly littered with wreckage and debris, making it difficult to navigate. Walk quickly and carefully, stay low to maintain visibility in smoke, and take care to avoid injuring yourself. Keep moving until you reach a safe place.

EMERGENCIES ON AN AIRPLANE

- **Stop**—Stay calm and remain in your seat with your lap belt fastened, unless you are in immediate danger from fire or other bodily hazards.

- **Look**—If you see an emergency or suspicious activity, notify a flight attendant or crew member immediately. The sooner trained personnel know about an emergency, the sooner they can act to bring the situation under control. If you see fire or smoke and you must move to avoid injury, stay low to maintain visibility.

- **Listen**—It is important that you follow the instructions of the flight attendant, the crew, or emergency personnel on the scene. If an evacuation is necessary, the flight attendant, the crew, or emergency service workers will help you exit the plane quickly and safely.

Before a Disaster

You should have a plan in case of an emergency and do your best to stay calm. Be advised that precautionary airplane evacuations occur about once every 11 days in the United States.

Panicked passengers are likely to create bottlenecks at doorways and emergency exits. Passengers could be trampled in these situations. Know your alternate escape routes, and do the following:

- Leave a copy of your itinerary with family or friends at home.

- Dress for survival. Wear long pants (not shorts or skirts) and tie-on shoes. Cover as much skin as possible (even at the expense of temporary comfort), but avoid restrictive clothing. Choose natural clothing fabrics like cotton, wool, or leather. Many man-made (synthetic) fabrics like polyester and rayon melt when exposed to flames (also avoid pantyhose).

- Before you board the plane, pay *very* close attention to your bags at all times. Do not accept packages from strangers. Do not pack anything in your carry-on that may be utilized as a weapon (including sports equipment).

- Be aware of your surroundings at all times (even in the parking lot, when you arrive at the airport). Report any suspicious behavior or activity (or unattended bags) to airport security or the gate attendant. Take stock of your fellow passengers in the terminal while you wait to board.

- If you are prepared to take on the responsibility, consider taking an exit-row seat. Pay close attention to the flight attendants' special instructions for exit-row passengers. Be advised that you may be called on to take a leadership role if an evacuation is required (be ready to use a command voice).

- Pay attention to the flight attendants' safety briefing. The flight attendants and the crew (and the "plain clothes" air marshall) are very highly trained in survival practices and emergency procedures.

- Also read the safety briefing card on every single flight. Each model of airplane has distinct safety features and different escape routes.

- Note where the emergency exits are located and how to operate the emergency release handles.

- Count the number of seats to the nearest emergency exit. Locate the nearest exits both in front of you *and* behind you.
- Note where the fire extinguisher is located, and consider how to remove it from the mounting bracket.
- Note where the first-aid kit is located.
- Locate the emergency flotation device (often the seat bottom).
- Place your carry-on baggage under the seat in front of you, and not in the overhead bin, to create a block so that your feet and legs cannot go up under the seat in front. Broken legs and feet make up a significant number of the injuries reported in an emergency landing situation.
- Wear your lap belt tightly at *all* times, unless you must get up to use the lavatory.
- Avoid alcohol and maintain a high state of alert and watchfulness.

During a Disaster

An airplane is a *very* safe means of transportation, and evacuations are very rarely necessary. However, emergencies do happen, and if it does become necessary to evacuate the plane, each passenger must know what to do. Remember to listen to the instructions given by the flight attendant, the crew, or emergency personnel who will tell you what to do. Additionally, follow these general rules:

- Obey the flight attendants' directions before an emergency, during a crisis, and after a crash.
- If time permits, review the safety information in the seat pocket in front of you.
- Protect your legs and feet. Plant your feet as far back as possible.
- Remove your eyeglasses and place them in a breast pocket or temporarily hang them from the collar of your shirt.
- Take pens and pencils (and other potentially dangerous items) out of your pockets.
- Brace yourself for an emergency landing:
  - If there is a seat in front of you, cross your hands on the seat in front of you and rest your forehead on top of your hands.
  - If you do not have a seat in front of you, bend over as far as you can, grab your legs behind your knees, and keep your head down until the plane stops.
- If the oxygen mask drops down, put it on yourself before helping someone else. In the worst case scenario, you may have only about 10 seconds to put your mask in place before you are rendered unconscious. If you are responsible for someone else, you need to take care of yourself first and then take care of the other person.
- Be courteous to others, and pay attention to the crew and emergency personnel.
- If fire and smoke are present and time permits, use wet paper towels or a handkerchief over your nose and mouth.
- Follow the floor-level exit lighting to an exit row. If fire and smoke are present, stay low to maintain visibility and to breathe fresh air.

- If you must to evacuate, leave your luggage and do not try to take *anything* with you. Items may get in the way of other passengers trying to evacuate or slow you down.
- When you are moving to the proper emergency exit, do not push or shove.
- Sometimes, flight crews are not able to provide direction. Know what to do in a crisis, even without the orders. Use common sense and sound judgment; you don't necessarily have to wait for orders to be able to evacuate.
- Using evacuation slides:
  - Jump feet first.
  - Do not sit down to slide.
  - Place your arms across your chest, tuck elbows in, and keep your legs and feet together.
  - Remove high-heel shoes.
- Be aware of debris and hazards around the plane and in your exit path. Look for downed power lines, hazardous material spills, leaking fuel, open flames, and so forth.
- Be aware of emergency vehicles.
- Walk directly to a safe area (at least 100 paces away) and remain there. Be sure to move upwind to avoid smoke.
- *Do not* return to the airplane for *any* reason.

After a Disaster Evacuation

Just because you are off of the plane does not mean that you can assume you are out of danger. As always, listen for instructions from the flight attendant, crew, or emergency personnel. Additionally, follow these guidelines:

- Be aware of debris and hazards around the plane and in your exit path. Look for downed power lines, hazardous material spills, leaking fuel, open flames, and so forth.
- Be aware of emergency vehicles.
- Walk directly to a safe area (at least 100 paces away) and remain there. Be sure to move upwind to avoid smoke.
- *Do not* return to the airplane for *any* reason.

Appendix F

Sheltering in Place

In an emergency, public health officials or local authorities may advise you to "shelter in place." You may receive these instructions via television or radio in the event of impending tornadoes or hurricanes, or where hazardous materials may have been released into the atmosphere. Sheltering in place is a precaution intended to keep you safe while remaining indoors. Be advised that this is not the same thing as retreating to a shelter in case of a storm. To shelter in place means selecting a small interior room, with few or no windows, and taking refuge there. It does not mean sealing off your entire home or office building.

When authorities issue the warning to shelter in place, there will be very little time for the public to make preparations. Generally, people do not respond instantly to a warning. Instead, people tend to seek out additional information from friends, relatives, neighbors, and the media. It will take anywhere from 15 to 40 minutes to tape and seal a room, and any delay in your reaction to the initial warning could result in your exposure to either an outdoor concentration prior to reaching a shelter environment or an outdoor concentration of hazardous material entering a structure before it is closed up.

TAKE PROTECTIVE MEASURES

The situation in your area may involve unique circumstances. Your local emergency planning committee or office of emergency services can provide you with details.

Before a Disaster

Unless otherwise instructed to evacuate, sheltering in a predetermined safe location in your home or place of work is the preferred method of safely waiting out many emergencies (particularly airborne hazardous materials). Sheltering in place usually lasts no more than one to two hours, and making preparations in advance can ensure that the event is as comfortable as possible for you and your family.

- Individuals with special needs may choose to or have to shelter in place during emergencies, and they should inform emergency officials about their situation before and during an event.
- Learn what fixed and mobile sources of hazardous materials are located in your vicinity. Look for chemical plants, nuclear power plants, universities equipped with nuclear reactors, active rail lines, major highways, and so forth.
- Learn about any warning sirens where you live and work. Your local emergency planning committee or office of emergency services can give you information about the sirens. Know when they are tested and for how long.
- Prepare a 72-hour (3 days) family disaster supplies kit appropriate for the type(s) of emergencies that could occur near you. The kit should contain duct tape for sealing cracks around doors and windows, and plastic (preferably, 10 mil or 0.01 inch, or about 0.25 mm, thickness and precut to size).
- If your house was built before 1950, consider weatherizing it. Based on the history of building codes and overall construction practices, homes constructed since the early to mid-1970s are likely to have significantly lower air infiltration rates than homes constructed prior to that time. Housing built before 1950 will likely be unsuitable for sheltering without weatherization.
- Check your disaster supplies kit every six months, and rotate food and water supplies.
- Select an interior room without windows that is located above ground level. In the case of a chemical threat, an above-ground location is preferable because some chemicals are heavier than air and may seep into basements even if the windows are closed. Alternatively (depending on the type of emergency, including tornadoes and hurricanes), select a secure place in your basement (consider a corner location without large heavy objects or appliances on the floor directly above you). Use sound judgment, and consider whether your basement could become a flood hazard (due to storm surges, etc.).
- Select a room with a telephone (though you should use it only for emergency calls) and a power outlet.
- Store emergency numbers in your cell phone(s) under "ICE" (In Case of Emergency).
- Consider using a stand-alone portable HEPA filter.
- Ask your school administrators or day-care providers about their training and preparations for an emergency. Reassure yourself that they know what to do to properly shelter in place and protect your children because you should *not* leave your home to get them when authorities issue the shelter-in-place advisory.

- Contact your local gas company for guidance on preparation and response regarding gas appliances and gas service to your home since there are different gas shutoff procedures for different gas meter configurations. When you learn the proper shutoff procedure for your meter, share the information with everyone in your household. Be sure you do not actually turn off the gas when practicing the proper gas shutoff procedure. Keep the tools necessary for shutting off the gas in the vicinity of your meter.

During a Disaster

If you are told to shelter in place, follow these guidelines:

At Home

- If you are outside, get inside immediately.
- Close and lock all windows and exterior doors.
- If you are told there is danger of an explosion, close the window shades, blinds, or curtains.
- Turn off all fans and heating and air-conditioning systems, and close the fireplace damper.
- Get your family disaster supplies kit, and make sure the radio is working.
- Shut off the gas at the outside main valve, if you can.
- Go to your preselected sheltering location.
- Bring your pets with you, and be sure to bring additional food and water supplies for them.
- Take your cellular phone and charger with you.
- Call your emergency contact, and have the phone available if you need to report a life-threatening condition. Cellular telephone equipment may be overwhelmed or damaged during an emergency.
- Use duct tape and plastic sheeting to seal all cracks around the door and any vents into the room.
- If you have one, turn on your portable HEPA air purifier/filter.
- Monitor your radio or television until you are told all is safe or you are told to evacuate. Local officials may call for evacuation in specific areas at greatest risk in your community.

At Work or School

- If you are outside, get inside immediately.
- If there are visitors in the building, provide for their safety by asking them to stay put.
- Call your family and your emergency contact on your cellular phone.
- Listen to instructions from trusted sources (for example, teachers in school or designated safety personnel at work) and proceed to a designated shelter location inside the building.

- Select interior room(s) above the ground floor with the fewest windows or vents. The room(s) should have adequate space for everyone to be able to sit in. Avoid overcrowding by selecting several rooms if necessary. Classrooms may be used if there are no windows or the windows are sealed and cannot be opened. Large storage closets, utility rooms, meeting rooms, and even a gymnasium without exterior windows will also work well.
- Help to close and lock all windows, exterior doors, and any other openings to the outside.
- If you are told there is danger of an explosion, help to close the window shades, blinds, or curtains.
- Have employees familiar with your building's mechanical systems turn off the gas and all fans and heating and air-conditioning systems. Be advised that some systems automatically provide for exchange of inside air with outside air, and these systems must be turned off, sealed, or disabled.
- Gather essential disaster supplies, such as nonperishable food, bottled water, battery-powered radios, first-aid supplies, flashlights, batteries, duct tape, plastic sheeting, and plastic garbage bags.
- Write down the names of everyone in the room, and call your school's or office's designated emergency contact to report the names of the students/people in the room with you.
- Monitor the radio, television, or communications with school officials until you are told all is safe or you are told to evacuate. Local officials may call for evacuation in specific areas at greatest risk in your community.

In Your Car

- If you are very close to home, your office, or a public building, go there immediately and get inside. Follow the shelter-in-place recommendations.
- If you cannot quickly and safely get to a home or building, then pull over to the side of the road. Stop your vehicle in the safest place possible. In the heat of the summer, try to stop under a bridge or find a shady spot.
- Turn off the engine and close windows and vents.
- If possible, seal the heating/ air-conditioning vents with duct tape.
- Call your family and your emergency contact on your cellular phone.
- Monitor the radio for updated advice and instructions.
- Stay where you are until you are told it is safe to get back on the road. Be aware that some roads may be closed.

Remember that instructions to shelter in place are usually provided for durations of a few hours, not days or weeks. There is little danger that the room in which you are taking shelter will run out of oxygen and that you will suffocate.

After a Disaster

When you hear the "all clear" message over the emergency broadcast system, you should do the following:

- Open doors and windows.
- Turn on your heating/cooling system to ventilate the house.
- Go outside (when the emergency is over, the concentration of hazardous material outside will likely be lower than the concentration that will accumulate in a closed house).
- Be aware of dangers, and watch for downed power lines, fallen trees, debris, and local wildlife that may pose a threat to you and your pet.
- Monitor your family members for any abnormal behavior or illness. Contact your doctor if you have any concerns.

Appendix G

Emergency Communications

Timely communication is critical in an emergency, and lives may hang in the balance. People will instinctively use their telephones to call 9-1-1 or to call family members to make sure they are safe. People will also monitor televisions and radios to get information updates about an event. Many will take these modern conveniences for granted, but unusual conditions can put a strain on the communications infrastructure. You should be prepared when the power goes out or the typical lines of communication are overwhelmed.

Store emergency numbers in your cell phone under "ICE" (In Case of Emergency) so that someone else can call your emergency numbers if you are incapacitated.

Be advised that if you use a cable modem or a digital subscriber line (DSL) to connect to the Internet, you may be able to access e-mail during an emergency, even if your standard telephone line is blocked due to congestion.

9-1-1

The 9-1-1 emergency services network was created in the United States more than 20 years ago as a fast and efficient way to access police and fire department services toll-free from almost any telephone or any cellular telephone (the 9-1-1 network still does not completely cover some rural areas of the United States and Canada). Most traditional wire line 9-1-1 systems now automatically report to the Public Safety Answering Point (PSAP) the telephone number and location of calls, a capability called Enhanced 9-1-1 (E911). The mobility of wireless telephone service makes determining a wireless user's location more complicated than is true for traditional wire line services, which are associated with a fixed location or address. The U.S. Federal Communications Commission (FCC) has adopted rules requiring wireless telephone carriers to provideE911, but the service will not be available everywhere immediately. Whenever you call 9--1-1, follow these general guidelines:

- Immediately tell the emergency operator the location of the emergency.
- Give the emergency operator your wireless phone number so that if the call gets disconnected, the operator can call you back.
- Even if you do not have a contract for service with a wireless service provider (i.e., your phone is not activated), you can use your cellular telephone for emergency 9-1-1 calls. However, if your emergency call gets disconnected, you must call the emergency operator back because he or she does not automatically receive your telephone number and cannot call you back.

In most countries outside the United States and Canada, 9-1-1 does not work. Internationally, the most common emergency numbers are 1-1-0, 1-1-2, and 9-9-9. In 1991, the European Union established 1-1-2 as the universal emergency number for all its member states. In most EU countries, 1-1-2 is already effective and can be called toll-free from any telephone or any cellular telephone. The GSM mobile phone standard designates 1-1-2 as an emergency number, so it will work on those systems even in the United States.

2-1-1

Many states have adopted 2-1-1 as an easy-to-remember telephone number that connects people with important community services and volunteer opportunities. The United Way is spearheading the implementation of 2-1-1 in cooperation with specialized regional information and referral agencies.

While the services offered through 2-1-1 vary from community to community, 2-1-1 provides callers with information about and referrals to human services for everyday needs and in times of crisis. For example, 2-1-1 can offer access to the following:

- **Basic Human Needs**—Referral to resources including food banks, clothing closets, shelters, rent assistance, utility assistance, and disaster/emergency information
- **Youth and Family Services**—Support for children, youth, and families, including child care, after-school programs, Head Start, family resource centers, summer camps and recreation programs, mentoring, tutoring, and protective services
- **Physical and Mental Health Resources**—Direction to health insurance programs, Medicaid and Medicare, maternal health, Children's Health Insurance Program, medical information lines, crisis intervention services, support groups, counseling, and drug and alcohol intervention and rehabilitation
- **Employment Support**—Referral to financial assistance, job training, transportation assistance, and education programs

- **Support for Older Americans and Persons with Disabilities**—Guidance to adult day care, congregate meals, Meals on Wheels, respite care, home health care, transportation, homemaker services
- **Volunteerism**—Direction to volunteer opportunities and donations

CITIZEN'S BAND (CB)

Today, Citizen's Band Radio is a system of short-distance radio communication between individuals on a selection of 40 channels within the single Very High Frequency (VHF) 27 megahertz (MHz; 11 meter) band. The CB radio service should not be confused with FRS, GMRS, MURS, or amateur radio. Similar personal radio services exist in other countries (generally between the 26 MHz and 28 MHz frequency bands), with varying requirements for licensing and differing technical standards. In many countries, CB does not require a license, and unlike amateur radio, it may be used for commercial communication.

Considerations

- There are no age, citizenship, or license requirements to operate a CB radio in the United States.
- Equipment output power is limited to 4 watts (W) for AM transmitters and 12 W PEP (peak envelope power) for single sideband (SSB) transmitters. Generally, the communications range is from one to five miles, or up to about eight km.
- *Channel 9 (27.065 MHz) is used only for emergency communications* or for traveler assistance.

49 MHZ PERSONAL RADIOS

Before the introduction of the Family Radio Service (FRS), manufacturers experienced some success selling personal radios that operated in the 49 MHz frequency band. These personal radios are attractive to some people because they draw very little power and users generally do not have to contend with multiple users on their frequency.

The FCC does not require a license to operate these devices, but they have limitations that make them impractical for most emergency communications, including:

- The communications range is limited to about a quarter mile, or about 0.4 km.
- Early cordless phones, baby monitors, older security systems, and some other devices share this frequency band (in some cases, this can cause so-called contention).

Even with the limitations, 49 MHz personal radios are very inexpensive and they could be useful for neighborhood watch organizations or communicating with family members (within your immediate neighborhood).

FAMILY RADIO SERVICE (FRS)

The Family Radio Service is an improved walkie-talkie system authorized in the United States since 1996. This personal radio service uses frequencies in the ultra-high-frequency (UHF) band (14 channels) and does not suffer from the interference effects associated with CB at 27 MHz, or the 49 MHz band also used by cordless phones, toys, and baby monitors. FRS uses frequency modulation (FM) instead of amplitude modulation (AM) and has a greater reliable range than license-free radios operating in the CB or 49 MHz bands. FRS should not be confused with MURS or amateur radio. Similar personal radio services exist in other countries, but technical standards and frequency bands may differ. Usually FCC-approved FRS equipment may not be used in other countries (except Canada and Mexico). In Europe, the PMR446 personal radio service uses eight channels in the 446 MHz frequency band with the same sort of licensing restriction as FRS. You cannot legally use an FRS radio in Europe or a PMR446 radio in the United States (the 446 MHz band is allocated to FCC-licensed amateur radio in the United States).

Considerations

- There are no license requirements to operate an FCC-approved FRS radio in the United States.
- Equipment output power is limited to 500 milliwatts (one-half W). Generally, the communications range is from one to three miles, or up to about five km.
- Channels 1 to 7 are shared with the General Mobile Radio Service (GMRS). A license is required for those channels only if the power output is over FRS limits, up to GMRS limits.
- Unlike standard CB radios, FRS radios frequently have provisions for using subaudible tone squelch (CTCSS) codes, filtering out unwanted chatter from other users on the same frequency. Though these codes are sometimes called privacy codes, they offer no protection from eavesdropping and are only intended to help share busy channels.
- In some communities, volunteer organizations *monitor Channel 1 (462.5625 MHz) for emergency communications.*

GENERAL MOBILE RADIO SERVICE (GMRS)

The General Mobile Radio Service (GMRS) is like the FRS in that it operates in the 460 MHz region (with up to 22 channels), uses small handheld transceivers, and is intended to be used by individuals to communicate with immediate family members. The big differences are that GMRS requires an FCC license with a fee and users must be 18 years or older. In addition, the output of these units is considerably greater (1 to 5 W), allowing a range of coverage from 5 to 25 miles, or up to about 40 km, depending on terrain and antenna position.

Considerations

- The FCC requires you to secure a license to *operate* (no license is required to purchase) an FCC-approved GMRS radio in the United States (including the popular FRS/GMRS hybrid units). When you secure an FCC license to operate a GMRS radio, your immediate family members, including a spouse, children, parents, grandparents, aunts, uncles, nephews, nieces, and in-laws are also authorized use it (contact the FCC for more information).

- Equipment output power is limited to 1 to 5 W. Generally, the communications range is from 5 to 20 miles, or up to about 32km.

- Channels 1 to 7 are shared with the Family Radio Service (FRS).

- Like FRS radios, GMRS radios frequently have provisions for using subaudible tone squelch (CTCSS) codes, filtering out unwanted chatter from other users on the same frequency. Though these codes are sometimes called privacy codes, they offer no protection from eavesdropping and are only intended to help share busy channels.

- Many GMRS radios also incorporate facilities for receiving National Oceanic and Atmospheric Administration (NOAA) weather alerts.

- *Channel 20 (467.675 MHz) is used for emergency communications* or for traveler assistance, and in some communities, volunteer organizations monitor *Channel 1 (462.5625 MHz) for emergency communications.*

MULTIUSE RADIO SERVICE (MURS)

The Multiuse Radio Service (MURS) is a small two-way radio service consisting of five frequencies in the VHF spectrum. Established by the FCC in the fall of 2000, MURS created a radio service allowing for unlicensed operation, with a power limit of 2 W, four times that of FRS radio.

Considerations

- There are no license requirements to operate an FCC-approved MURS radio in the United States.

- Equipment output power is limited to 2 W. Generally, the communications range is about five miles, or about eight km.

- MURS operates in the 151 MHz and 154 MHz frequency bands (154 MHz is part of the FCC-regulated business band).

AMATEUR RADIO SERVICE (HAM RADIO)

Amateur radio or (Ham radio) is used by hobbyists and public service volunteers. Many Ham operators support the larger public community with emergency and disaster communications, especially when wire line and other conventional means of communications fail. Ham radio operators who are involved in emergency communications often belong to a national emergency club, such as the Amateur Radio Emergency Service (ARES) and the Radio Amateur Civil Emergency Service (RACES) in the United States or the Radio

Amateurs' Emergency Network (RAYNET) in the United Kingdom (UK). In areas at risk of severe storms and tornadoes, including the Midwestern and southern states in the United States, storm-watching groups such as SKYWARN coordinate Ham radio operators in the roles of storm spotters and chasers. These storm spotters and chasers report hazards to the National Weather Service to warn the general public of severe weather conditions.

The amateur radio high bands are the VHF, UHF, and microwave frequencies above 30 MHz. These bands typically allow radio amateurs to communicate locally. Voice transmissions are the most common way Ham operators communicate with one another, using frequency modulation (FM) offering high-quality audio for local operation where signals are strong, and others such as single sideband (SSB) for more reliable communications using a smaller bandwidth when signals are marginal. Generally, Ham operators use the shortwave bands (HF) for worldwide communication and the VHF and UHF bands for excellent regional communication. The two-meter band (144–148 MHz) is generally considered to be the most popular amateur radio band.

All Ham operators and their stations must be licensed by the FCC. To receive a license, you must pass a written exam. A nationwide system of repeaters on the 144 MHz and 440 MHz bands allows nearly seamless communications around the country. The entry-level Technician class license allows the user to operate (among others) in the two-meter band. Small two-meter handheld units are relatively inexpensive and provide a range of 20 to 50 miles, or up to about 80 km, depending on terrain, power, and the use of a repeater. Many repeaters also provide access to 9-1-1 services.

Considerations

- The FCC requires you to secure a license to operate an amateur radio in the United States.
- Many Ham operators support the larger public community with emergency and disaster communications.
- Generally, the communications range for small two-meter handheld units is about 20 to 50 miles, or up to about 80 km.
- The two-meter band (144–148 MHz) is generally considered to be the most popular amateur radio band.

SCANNERS

A scanner is a radio receiver that automatically tunes, or scans, two or more discrete frequencies. Generally, scanners cover the nonbroadcast radio bands between 30 MHz and 950 MHz using FM, although there are models that cover more of the radio spectrum and use other modulation types. In the UK, it is illegal to listen to almost anything outside the amateur radio and broadcast bands.

Modern scanners allow you to store multiple frequencies in memory so that you can quickly and easily tune in to local police communications or emergency responder communications traffic. Some even allow you to scan the specific DCS or CTCSS code used on a particular frequency if it is utilized by multiple operators. Additionally, most scanners receive a weather radio band so that you can monitor weather radio broadcasts.

Be advised that some local law enforcement organizations encrypt their communications, and additionally, some use so-called frequency hopping or trunking transceivers (parts of a single conversation can take place across multiple frequencies while the intended transceivers in the group are kept in sync). Generally, trunking systems operate in the 400 MHz, 700 MHz, or 800 MHz frequency bands. Some high-end scanners can receive these trunked communications.

GLOBAL POSITIONING SYSTEM (GPS)

The Global Positioning System, usually called GPS, is the only fully functional satellite navigation system. A constellation of more than two dozen GPS satellites broadcasts precise timing signals by radio, allowing any GPS receiver (abbreviated to GPSr) to accurately determine its location (longitude, latitude, and altitude) anywhere on Earth. The Wide Area Augmentation System (WAAS) makes compatible GPS receivers accurate to within two meters.

An increasing number of automobiles are equipped with GPS receivers, either at the time of manufacture or as aftermarket equipment, to assist drivers in finding their way in areas with which they are unfamiliar. Units with integrated moving map displays are mounted on or near the dashboard of the automobile and provide continuous information on the automobile's current position, speed, direction of travel, as well as information on nearby streets and landmarks. Many of these GPS navigation aids also allow the operator to save routes for retrieval at a later time.

Consideration

- Plan multiple evacuation routes to use in the event of an emergency and preprogram these routes into a GPS navigation tool.

EMERGENCY ALERT SYSTEM (EAS)

In the event of an emergency, many people rely on local radio or television stations to receive updates on what is happening and what to do. The Emergency Alert System (EAS) is a nationwide broadcast system put in place to disseminate timely information to the public about large-scale disasters. EAS currently enables the president and national, state, and local authorities to provide emergency information to the general public via broadcast, cable, and wireless cable systems. All entertainment radio and television broadcast stations (including digital television [DTV] broadcasters, digital cable television providers, digital broadcast radio, Digital Audio Radio Service [DARS], and Direct Broadcast Satellite [DBS] systems) and cable systems must broadcast emergency alerts and messages for national security emergencies initiated by the president.

EAS participants are not required to broadcast EAS alerts and messages initiated by state and local authorities, but the FCC encourages them to transmit emergency alerts as a public service. Information about local natural disasters is often broadcast via EAS.

EMERGENCY WEATHER RECEIVERS

NOAA Weather Radio All Hazards is a network of radio stations broadcasting continuous weather information directly from a nearby National Weather Service (NWS) office. It is operated by the NWS, an agency of NOAA within the U.S. Department of Commerce. NOAA Weather Radio (NWR) broadcasts National Weather Service warnings, watches, forecasts, and other hazard information 24 hours a day. It also broadcasts alerts of nonweather emergencies such as national security, natural, environmental, and public safety through the FCC's EAS. Newer radios can detect a digital-over-audio protocol called Specific Area Message Encoding (SAME), which allows the radio to limit alarms to certain warnings and just to the local broadcast area.

A number of manufacturers make hand-crank emergency receivers that you can include in your family disaster supplies kit. You can charge these radios by turning a hand crank, and they can be indispensable in the event of an emergency or a power outage.

PERSONAL LOCATOR BEACONS (PLB)

On July 1, 2003, the FCC authorized the use of Personal Locator Beacons (PLBs). PLBs will provide a distress and alerting capacity for use by the general public in life-threatening situations in remote environments after all other means of notifying Search and Rescue (SAR) responders (for example, telephone and radio) have been exhausted. If you are involved in an emergency and you are out of cell phone range, a PLB, which is a small transmitter that sends out a personalized emergency distress signal, is a highly effective and internationally recognized way to summon help.

PLBs transmit distress signals on 406 MHz, which is an internationally recognized distress frequency, to the COSPAS-SARSAT satellite system. This international program includes the support and cooperation of 36 nations. In the United States, the 406 MHz signal is monitored by NOAA and the Air Force Rescue Coordination Center (AFRCC). Once a signal is received, the satellites can fix on the signal using a Doppler Shift location method or GPS (when a PLB is hooked up to a GPS). The signal is then relayed to a Local

User Terminal (LUT). These small satellite tracking stations are located all over the world and provide the link between the satellites and the Mission Control Center (MCC). In the United States, the NOAA serves as the MCC. This signal is then passed on to the Air Force to begin the Search and Rescue procedures.

Each PLB is equipped with a unique identifying code, which is a 15-digit alphanumeric code. This code is transmitted in the electronic burst to the satellites and is linked to a computer data base maintained by NOAA to provide your name, address, phone number, and any pertinent information such as medical problems to Search and Rescue personnel.

EMERGENCY FAMILY COMMUNICATIONS PLAN

Complete a contact card, like the sample below, for each family member. Have family members keep these cards handy in a wallet, purse, or backpack. You may want to send one to school with each child to keep on file. Pick a friend or relative who lives out of state for household members to notify when they are safe.

Hospital(s) near home/work: ______
Pharmacy/phone no.: ______
Health insurance/phone no.: ______
Physician name(s)/phone no.(s): ______
Past/current medical conditions: ______
Current medications/dosages: ______
Allergies: ______
Birth year: ______ Height: ______ Weight: ______ Blood type: ______

Critical Personal Medical Information

FOLD ← → FOLD

Emergency Family Communications Plan

My name: ______ Emergency contact: ______
My phone no.: ______ Phone no.: ______
Dial 9-1-1 for emergencies! Out-of-town contact: ______
Phone no.: ______
Neighborhood meeting place/phone no.: ______
Regional meeting place/phone no.: ______
School/phone no.: ______
State public health dept./phone no.: ______

Figure G.1: Example Contact Card, Emergency Family Communications Plan

Index

About the Author

JAMES (JAY) SCHAEFER-JONES is director of night vision programs for a government subcontractor in Fairfield, New Jersey, where he supports a domestic and international network of sales representatives responsible for night vision and security product sales to military, federal, local law enforcement, and broadcast and media customers. He is an active volunteer with his local Radio Amateur Civil Emergency Service (RACES) and Community Emergency Response Team (CERT). An engineer by training, he also served in the United States Marine Corps as a chief communications and electronics technician at Camp LeJeune, North Carolina, writing standard operating procedures (SOPs) and operator's manuals. He was formally recognized through official correspondence for improvising unique solutions during Operations Desert Shield and Desert Storm.